TYPE 2 DIABETIC

AIR FRYER COOKBOOK FOR THE NEWLY DIAGNOSED

800 DAYS LOW FAT, LOW SUGAR & LOW CARB RECIPES WITH 21-DAY MEAL PLAN TO EAT ON A HEALTHY DIET AND LIVE WELL WITH TYPE 2 DIABETES

MIRANDA NAQUIN

Copyright © 2021 by Miranda Naquin All rights reserved.

The content contained within this book may not be reproduced, duplicated, or transmitted without direct written permission from the author or the publisher. Under no circumstances will any blame or legal responsibility be held against the publisher, or author, for any damages, reparation, or monetary loss due to the information contained within this book, either directly or indirectly.

Legal Notice: This book is copyright protected. It is only for personal use. You cannot amend, distribute, sell, use, quote or paraphrase any part, or the content within this book, without the consent of the author or publisher.

Disclaimer Notice: Please note the information contained within this document is for educational and entertainment purposes only. All effort has been executed to present accurate, up to date, reliable, complete information. No warranties of any kind are declared or implied. Readers acknowledge that the author is not engaged in the rendering of legal, financial, medical, or professional advice. The content within this book has been derived from various sources. Please consult a licensed professional before attempting any techniques outlined in this book. By reading this document, the reader agrees that under no circumstances is the author responsible for any losses, direct or indirect, that are incurred as a result of the use of the information contained within this document, including, but not limited to, errors, omissions, or inaccuracies.

TABLE OF CONTENTS

BASICS ABOUT THE TYPE 2 DIABETIC DIET ..5
USING THE AIR FRYER..................................8
21-DAY MEAL PLAN 12

POULTRY RECIPES 14
- Teriyaki Chicken Legs..............................14
- Air-fried Turkey Breast With Cherry Glaze 15
- Poblano Bake..16
- Apricot Glazed Chicken Thighs 17
- Quick Chicken For Filling 18
- Peanut Butter-barbeque Chicken 19
- Italian Roasted Chicken Thighs 20
- Tandoori Chicken Legs.............................21
- Lemon Sage Roast Chicken 22
- Chicken Adobo..23

VEGETABLE SIDE DISHES

RECIPES 24
- Perfect Broccoli 24
- Roasted Cauliflower With Garlic And Capers 25
- Perfect Broccolini 26
- Tandoori Cauliflower................................27
- Tomato Candy 28
- Roasted Garlic And Thyme Tomatoes........29
- Simple Roasted Sweet Potatoes...............30
- Cauliflower 30
- Shoestring Butternut Squash Fries 31
- Charred Radicchio Salad.........................32
- Roasted Peppers With Balsamic Vinegar And Basil..33
- Sweet Potato Curly Fries 34
- Roasted Yellow Squash And Onions 35
- Crispy Brussels Sprouts 36
- Blistered Tomatoes..................................37

Fried Cauliflower With Parmesan Lemon Dressing..38
- Roman Artichokes...................................39
- Onions 40
- Mushrooms, Sautéed...............................41

APPETIZERS AND SNACKS....................42
- Carrot Chips 42
- Okra Chips 43
- Crispy Spiced Chickpeas 44
- Warm And Salty Edamame......................45
- Kale Chips 46
- Halloumi Fries 47
- Cinnamon Apple Crisps...........................48
- Crispy Tofu Bites 49
- Zucchini Chips..50
- Chicken Shawarma Bites 51
- Garlic Parmesan Kale Chips 52
- Za'atar Garbanzo Beans 52
- Baba Ghanouj 53
- Blistered Shishito Peppers 54
- Green Olive And Mushroom Tapenade 55
- Roasted Red Pepper Dip.........................56

BREAD AND BREAKFAST 57
- Goat Cheese, Beet, And Kale Frittata 57
- Mexican-style Roasted Corn....................58
- Roasted Vegetable Frittata......................59
- Sweet Potato-cinnamon Toast..................60
- Baked Eggs..60

FISH AND SEAFOOD RECIPES 61
- Salmon Puttanesca En Papillotte With Zucchini..61
- Garlic And Dill Salmon.............................62

Shrimp "scampi" 63
Lemon-roasted Salmon Fillets 64
Buttery Lobster Tails 65
Butternut Squash–wrapped Halibut Fillets 66
Black Cod With Grapes, Fennel, Pecans And Kale 67
Cajun Flounder Fillets 68
Blackened Red Snapper 69
Easy Scallops With Lemon Butter 70
Italian Tuna Roast 71
Pecan-crusted Tilapia 72
Sesame-crusted Tuna Steaks 73
Sweet Potato–wrapped Shrimp 74
Blackened Catfish 75
Lobster Tails With Lemon Garlic Butter 76
Five Spice Red Snapper With Green Onions And Orange Salsa 77
Quick Shrimp Scampi 78
Crab Stuffed Salmon Roast 79

VEGETARIANS RECIPES 80
Vegetable Couscous 80
Lentil Fritters 81
Pizza Portobello Mushrooms 82
Veggie Fried Rice 83

BEEF, PORK & LAMB RECIPES 84
Beef And Spinach Braciole 84
Almond And Sun-dried Tomato Crusted Pork Chops 85
Pork Chops 86
Rosemary Lamb Chops 86
Carne Asada 87
Barbecue-style London Broil 88
Lemon-butter Veal Cutlets 89
Perfect Pork Chops 90
Balsamic Marinated Rib Eye Steak With Balsamic Fried Cipollini Onions 91
Beef Al Carbon (street Taco Meat) 92
Mustard-crusted Rib-eye 92
Pesto-rubbed Veal Chops 93
Boneless Ribeyes 94
Lamb Chops 95
Tuscan Veal Chops 96
Garlic And Oregano Lamb Chops 97
Marinated Rib-eye Steak With Herb Roasted Mushrooms 98
Pork Loin 99
T-bone Steak With Roasted Tomato, Corn And Asparagus Salsa 100
Cinnamon-stick Kofta Skewers 101
Flank Steak With Roasted Peppers And Chimichurri 102
Lollipop Lamb Chops With Mint Pesto 103
Venison Backstrap 104
Perfect Strip Steaks 105
Smokehouse-style Beef Ribs 106
Peppered Steak Bites 107
Lamb Koftas Meatballs 108

BASICS ABOUT THE TYPE 2 DIABETIC DIET

1. Know the Type 2 Diabetes

Your body can't hold blood sugar regularly if you have type 2 diabetes because it doesn't use insulin properly. Type 2 diabetes affects 90-95 percent of diabetics. It takes several years to develop and is commonly diagnosed in adults (but more in children, teens, and young adults). Since you may not have any signs, it's crucial to get your blood sugar checked if you're in danger.

1. What Type 2 Diabetes is

Type 2 diabetes is a severe disorder in which the pancreas' insulin does not function properly or does not produce enough insulin. This indicates that the blood glucose (sugar) levels continue to rise.

2. Factors Contribute to the Development of Type 2 Diabetes

Insulin is needed for our survival. It serves an important purpose. It allows blood glucose to reach our cells and provide energy to our bodies.

Your body also breaks down carbohydrates from food and drinks and converts them to glucose if you have type 2 diabetes. The pancreas then releases insulin in response to this. However, since this insulin cannot function properly, the blood sugar levels continue to rise. More insulin is produced as a result of this.

3. Type 2 Diabetes isn't Curable

While there is no cure for type 2 diabetes, certain people can get remission. This indicates that your blood sugar levels are normal and that you no longer need diabetes medication. Remission may be life-changing, but it isn't always possible.

4. Type 2 Diabetes Treatments

Type 2 diabetes can be treated in various ways, including making healthier lifestyle decisions, using insulin, or taking medication. Your healthcare team will assist you in determining the best treatment option for you. This will help you live well with diabetes by lowering the risk of complications.

2. Treating Type 2 Diabetes

Managing your diabetes can often feel like walking a tight rope without a net. For some, it becomes a daily struggle to maintain a healthy glucose level, no matter how hard they try. Your blood sugar can drop, or spike, depending on several different factors.

Since the body is still producing some insulin, conventional treatments for type 2 diabetes focus on diet and exercise. Most people don't understand the effects that stress has on the body, and it can even cause your blood sugar to increase or decrease. The most common treatment for diabetes is insulin therapy. So let's look at each of these elements and see how they can benefit you.

1. Healthy Eating

Many people assume that overeating sugar is the reason their glucose levels are too high. But they are wrong. While paying attention to how much sugar you eat is essential, it is more important to keep track of the carbohydrates you consume.

Our bodies turn all carbohydrates into sugar for fuel. So while you may think a particular food is okay, since it doesn't have a lot of sugar, it may be high in carbs and cause your blood sugar to soar. But for now, just know that a healthy diet which pays attention to carbohydrate levels is one of the best ways to manage Type 2 Diabetes.

2. Exercise and Diabetes

Exercise, along with a healthy diet, can help you to keep your blood sugar in a healthy range. You don't need to run out and buy an expensive gym membership or any fancy equipment. You need to follow a simple, easy exercise routine. Most importantly, you need to be consistent, whatever exercise you choose, make sure you do it every day.

Since Type 2 diabetes is most often found in adults who are overweight and tend to be sedimentary, simply walking every day can be beneficial. When your blood sugar is too high, a casual stroll around the neighborhood can help bring it down to a reasonable level again. Start small if you must, get up and move more throughout your day.

3. Energy Nutrients for the Type 2 Diabetic Diet

1. Carbohydrates

Dietary carbohydrates from cereals, bread, other grain products, legumes, vegetables, fruits, dairy products, and added sugars should provide the most significant portion of an individual's energy requirements—both the amount consumed and the source of carbohydrate influence blood glucose and insulin responses. The terms "simple" and "complex" should not be used to classify carbohydrates because they do not help determine their impact on blood glucose levels.

Beyond the chemical composition, other factors such as Ingested particle size, food form, starch structure, and cooking methods may affect the carbohydrate digestion rate from the small intestine and the blood glucose response.

2. Sugars

In the past, sugar avoidance has been one of the significant nutritional advice for people with diabetes. However, research has shown that sugars are an integral part of a healthy diet for diabetes, especially sugar gotten from vegetables, fruits, and dairy products. Added sugars, for example, sugar-sweetened and table sugar products, make up around 10% of the day-to-day energy needs. Foods containing sugars vary in physiological effects and nutritional value. For example, sucrose and squeezed orange juice have comparative blood glucose effects but contain different nutrients and minerals. Consuming whole fruits and fruit juices causes blood glucose concentrations to peak slightly earlier but fall more quickly than consuming an equal carbohydrate portion of white bread.

Refined sucrose gives a lower blood glucose reaction than many refined starches. Some improved breakfast cereals produce lower plasma glucose and insulin reaction than equivalent carbohydrate portions of unsweetened cereals. Thus, unnecessary avoidance of foods containing simple sugars is not required. Notwithstanding, intake of added sucrose or high-fructose corn syrup and fructose over 10% of energy should be avoided since available evidence suggests that this may increase LDL cholesterol and/or serum triglycerides in susceptible people.

3. Protein

Current proof demonstrates individuals with diabetes have comparative protein prerequisites to those of everybody. Even though protein is essential for stimulating insulin secretion, excess consumption may add to the pathogenesis of diabetic nephropathy.

4. Fats

Various studies indicate high-fat weight control diet can weaken glucose resistance and cause atherosclerotic heart disease, dyslipidemia, and obesity. Research likewise shows these equivalent metabolic anomalies are managed or improved by reducing saturated fat intake. Current suggestions on fat intake for everyone apply equally to individuals with diabetes. Reducing the intake of saturated fat by 10% or less and cholesterol intake to 300 mg/d or less.

The research proposes monounsaturated fat (like canola, olive, and nut oils) may positively affect fatty oils and glycemic control in certain people with diabetes. Still, care should be taken to avoid excess weight gain. Omega-3 unsaturated fats, found in fish like mackerel and salmon, may decrease serum fatty oils without hindering glycemic control. Although consuming a huge amount of omega-3 unsaturated fats from natural food is likely, not practical for most, eating rich in omega-3 unsaturated fats at least once a week is recommended. On the other hand, ingesting trans-unsaturated fats usually found in many processed foods should be restricted. Vegetable oil produced by hydrogenating trans-unsaturated fats' organic effects is similar to those of saturated fat.

USING THE AIR FRYER

1. Reasons We Like the Air Fryer

1.   It produces real food Since it's essentially a small convection oven, the air fryer can cook many of the foods you might roast or bake with less fuss. The basket's wire base helps food to cook evenly since air circulates on all sides.

2.   Less-fat frying Yes, the air fryer's intended purpose holds true: Instead of quarts of oil, we can use just a small amount and achieve beautifully crisp results for French fries, chicken, fish, and more.

3.   Set and (almost) forget Unlike stovetop cooking, air frying requires virtually no monitoring, thanks to its well-regulated temperature and automatic shutoff. Other than the occasional flip or toss, it does all the work, allowing you to focus on the rest of the meal.

4.   Minimal mess The food basket is enclosed in the air fryer, and this translates to a clean kitchen—no splattering oil or multiple dirty pots and pans. Plus, the baskets are simple to clean—most are nonstick and dishwasher-safe.

5.   No stove—or oven—needed On busy nights when we must convince ourselves to cook (even test cooks feel this way at times), not having to turn on the stove can be a blessing. And on hot nights, the air fryer keeps our kitchen from becoming a steam room.

6.   It's fast The air fryer lets us skip past the common first step in cooking—heating fat in a pan or heating the oven or grill. This not only was convenient but also shaved valuable time off of our recipes.

7.   Easy meals for kids The ability to crisp up a batch of chicken nuggets, bake a couple of hand pies, or roast carrots without embarking on a cooking project makes this a lifesaver for busy parents.

8.   Ideal for two people When it's just the two of you eating (or you're cooking solo) and you don't want to make more than you need, the air fryer helps to prevent waste. Our recipes were made with standard air-fryer basket sizes in mind, and many yield two servings.

9.   Your automated sous chef Cooking multiple dishes in the oven can be a juggling act. Hand a side dish over to the air fryer and free up valuable space.

10.   Even results All of the previous benefits would amount to null if the air fryer's cooking results were spotty, but we continued to be surprised at how good the food tasted. The most common remark we heard at recipe tastings was, "I can't believe this came from an air fryer!"

2. How to Use the Air Fryer

An air fryer is basically a miniature convection oven: A fan blows heated air over food to cook it quickly. Here are the keys to using it well.

1. If your air fryer is new, clean it. Remove the basket and pan along with any accessories, and wash them with soap and water. Use a damp paper towel to clean the outside and inside of the air fryer. Dry off all of the components, and familiarize yourself with the instructions.

2. Prepare your food. Cut food into similar-size pieces so they cook evenly. If you want to marinate food, plan ahead. (Most foods only need to marinate for a few minutes, but for really deep flavor, you may want to marinate overnight in the refrigerator.) Then, pat the pieces dry. Any excess liquid on foods will drip into the pan and may cause the appliance to smoke.

3. If needed, preheat. Some air fryer models require preheating; others do not. Read the instruction manual for your appliance.

4. If you are going to coat food with crumbs, make sure that the coating is patted firmly onto the food. Spray other foods lightly with cooking spray or oil from a mister. Then, put the food into the basket or baking pan.

5. If you are going to use a pan, use the size recommended by the instruction manual. Most air fryers use a 6-by-6-by-2-inch pan, and the recipes in this book were developed for that size. Spray the pan with nonstick cooking spray, or line it with parchment paper liners that come with tabs to easily remove food. You can also use a 6-inch metal bowl as long it fits easily in the basket with room to spare on the top. The metal will be very hot, so to remove the pan or bowl, use spring-loaded tongs.

6. Place the basket into the air fryer and set the time. Don't overcrowd food in the basket. If you're cooking small items, such as tater tots or chopped vegetables, shake the food halfway through the cooking time. Remove the basket with the pan attached, and shake gently to redistribute the food. Some recipes ask you to turn food. Never use your fingers; use tongs or a large fork for this step.

7. When the food is done, remove the basket, with the pan in it, if used, and take the food out with tongs. Never tip the basket with the pan attached into a dish; any liquids or grease in the pan will spill onto the food and may burn your fingers.

3. Tips for Perfect Air Frying
The following 10 tips will help any new air fryer user. I find that they are the most common problems and questions that arise as you first use your air fryer.

1. Don't use aerosol spray.
One of the most common questions I come across is whether to use aerosol spray in your air fryer. The answer is no. Do not use any aerosol sprays in your air fryer, because they are usually lower quality oil and have additives such as propellants, which can damage your basket. As a result, the coating could come off. And, unfortunately, the coating could come off on your food, making it unsafe to eat. Therefore, before placing your food into the air fryer, simply give it a quick spray of olive oil.

2. Shake the basket frequently.
If you are making diced potatoes, diced chicken, or anything cut up into pieces, remember to shake the basket frequently. This shaking will guarantee the food is evenly cooked, evenly colored, and crispy. All you need to do is pull out the air fryer drawer, give it a few shakes, and put it back in.

3. Check the temperature and time.
Use the recommendations in the recipes and the charts as you start using your air fryer. But keep in mind that every model is different, so as you make new things, note the time it takes your machine to fully cook the food. Use a food thermometer to check for doneness. It is very dangerous to eat uncooked meat, especially pork and chicken.

4. Flip baked goods if the middle does not fully cook.
When you're baking quick breads, muffins, cakes, and other baked goods, if a toothpick test reveals that the middle isn't done yet at the end of the cook time, just take the bread, cake, etc., out of the pan and flip it. Carefully place it in the basket upside-down and allow it to finish cooking.

5. Spray generously with oil to avoid white spots on breaded foods.
White spots mean that you have not oiled your food enough; this happens on breaded food items.

6. Use your air fryer to heat frozen foods.
The air fryer is a great way to heat up your frozen foods; the general rule is a 30 percent reduction in time.

7. Don't overcrowd the air fryer basket.
If you start to get unevenly cooked food, the problem probably lies with the quantity of food you are making. You need to leave space between food items and not stack the food. Crowding and stacking result in food that cooks unevenly or lacks crispness.

8. Avoid smoke when cooking bacon.
If you get smoke when you are cooking bacon, put a slice of bread on the bottom of the drawer, which will absorb the grease and eliminate the smoking from the air fryer.

9. Use aluminum foil.
Foil is allowed in the air fryer. You can wrap vegetables in foil to steam them, or use it over baked goods, like cakes and pies, to slow browning on the top while the middle cooks.

10. Use parchment paper.
Using parchment paper really helps with cleanup, because you throw it away after use. Perforated parchment paper cut to fit many sizes of air fryer baskets is available. I have not been able to find it in box stores, but it is available on Amazon.

21-DAY MEAL PLAN

Meal Plan	Breakfast	Lunch	Dinner
Day-1	Goat Cheese, Beet, And Kale Frittata	Teriyaki Chicken Legs	Perfect Broccoli
Day-2	Mexican-style Roasted Corn	Garlic And Dill Salmon	Roasted Cauliflower With Garlic And Capers
Day-3	Roasted Vegetable Frittata	Air-fried Turkey Breast With Cherry Glaze	Fried Cauliflower With Parmesan Lemon Dressing
Day-4	Sweet Potato-cinnamon Toast	Shrimp "scampi"	Blistered Tomatoes
Day-5	Baked Eggs	Beef And Spinach Braciole	Tandoori Cauliflower
Day-6	Veggie Fried Rice	Buttery Lobster Tails	Roasted Garlic And Thyme Tomatoes
Day-7	Garlic Parmesan Kale Chips	Lemon-roasted Salmon Fillets	Roasted Yellow Squash And Onions
Day-8	Pizza Portobello Mushrooms	Butternut Squash–wrapped Halibut Fillets	Charred Radicchio Salad
Day-9	Vegetable Couscous	Apricot Glazed Chicken Thighs	Lentil Fritters
Day-10	Carrot Chips	Black Cod With Grapes, Fennel, Pecans And Kale	Mushrooms, Sautéed
Day-11	Goat Cheese, Beet, And Kale Frittata	Quick Chicken For Filling	Crispy Brussels Sprouts

21-DAY MEAL PLAN

Day-12	Crispy Tofu Bites	Almond And Sun-dried Tomato Crusted Pork Chops	Veggie Fried Rice
Day-13	Baked Eggs	Peanut Butter-barbeque Chicken	Shoestring Butternut Squash Fries
Day-14	Charred Radicchio Salad	Crab Stuffed Salmon Roast	Simple Roasted Sweet Potatoes
Day-15	Perfect Broccoli	Sesame-crusted Tuna Steaks	T-bone Steak With Roasted Tomato, Corn And Asparagus Salsa
Day-16	Tandoori Cauliflower	Italian Roasted Chicken Thighs	Sweet Potato Curly Fries
Day-17	Mexican-style Roasted Corn	Pork Chops	Lamb Chops
Day-18	Blistered Tomatoes	Tandoori Chicken Legs	Butternut Squash–wrapped Halibut Fillets
Day-19	Sweet Potato Curly Fries	Five Spice Red Snapper With Green Onions And Orange Salsa	Balsamic Marinated Rib Eye Steak With Balsamic Fried Cipollini Onions
Day-20	Shoestring Butternut Squash Fries	Lemon Sage Roast Chicken	Buttery Lobster Tails
Day-21	Sweet Potato-cinnamon Toast	Italian Tuna Roast	Crab Stuffed Salmon Roast

POULTRY RECIPES

Teriyaki Chicken Legs

Servings: 2
Cooking Time: 20 Minutes

Ingredients:
- 4 tablespoons sugar-free teriyaki sauce
- 1 tablespoon fresh orange juice
- 1 teaspoon smoked paprika
- 4 chicken legs
- cooking spray

Directions:

1. Mix together the teriyaki sauce, orange juice, and smoked paprika. Brush on all sides of chicken legs.
2. Spray air fryer basket with nonstick cooking spray and place chicken in basket.
3. Cook at 360°F for 6minutes. Turn and baste with sauce. Cook for 6 more minutes, turn and baste. Cook for 8 minutes more, until juices run clear when chicken is pierced with a fork.

Nutrition Info: Calories per serving: 439; Carbohydrates: 1.7g; Protein: 66.7g; Fat: 16.9g; Sugar: 0.4g; Sodium: 495mg; Fiber: 0.2g

Air-fried Turkey Breast With Cherry Glaze

Servings: 6
Cooking Time: 54 Minutes

Ingredients:

- 1 (5-pound) turkey breast
- 2 teaspoons olive oil
- 1 teaspoon dried thyme
- ½ teaspoon dried sage
- 1 teaspoon salt
- ½ teaspoon freshly ground black pepper
- ½ cup sugar-free cherry preserves
- 1 tablespoon chopped fresh thyme leaves
- 1 teaspoon low-sodium soy sauce*
- freshly ground black pepper

Directions:

1. All turkeys are built differently, so depending on the turkey breast and how your butcher has prepared it, you may need to trim the bottom of the ribs in order to get the turkey to sit upright in the air fryer basket without touching the heating element. The key to this recipe is getting the right size turkey breast. Once you've managed that, the rest is easy, so make sure your turkey breast fits into the air fryer basket before you Preheat the air fryer.
2. Preheat the air fryer to 350°F.
3. Brush the turkey breast all over with the olive oil. Combine the thyme, sage, salt and pepper and rub the outside of the turkey breast with the spice mixture.
4. Transfer the seasoned turkey breast to the air fryer basket, breast side up, and air-fry at 350°F for 25 minutes. Turn the turkey breast on its side and air-fry for another 12 minutes. Turn the turkey breast on the opposite side and air-fry for 12 more minutes. The internal temperature of the turkey breast should reach 165°F when fully cooked.
5. While the turkey is air-frying, make the glaze by combining the cherry preserves, fresh thyme, soy sauce and pepper in a small bowl. When the cooking time is up, return the turkey breast to an upright position and brush the glaze all over the turkey. Air-fry for a final 5 minutes, until the skin is nicely browned and crispy. Let the turkey rest, loosely tented with foil, for at least 5 minutes before slicing and serving.

Nutrition Info: Calories per serving: 430; Carbohydrates: 7g; Protein: 93.9g; Fat: 3.1g; Sugar: 0g; Sodium: 384mg; Fiber: 0.1g

Poblano Bake

Servings: 4
Cooking Time: 11 Minutes Per Batch

Ingredients:
- 2 large poblano peppers (approx. 5½ inches long excluding stem)
- ¾ pound ground turkey, raw
- ¾ cup cooked brown rice
- 1 teaspoon chile powder
- ½ teaspoon ground cumin
- ½ teaspoon garlic powder
- 4 ounces sharp Cheddar cheese, grated
- 1 8-ounce jar salsa, warmed

Directions:
1. Slice each pepper in half lengthwise so that you have four wide, flat pepper halves.
2. Remove seeds and membrane and discard. Rinse inside and out.
3. In a large bowl, combine turkey, rice, chile powder, cumin, and garlic powder. Mix well.
4. Divide turkey filling into 4 portions and stuff one into each of the 4 pepper halves. Press lightly to pack down.
5. Place 2 pepper halves in air fryer basket and cook at 390°F for 10 minutes or until turkey is well done.
6. Top each pepper half with ¼ of the grated cheese. Cook 1 more minute or just until cheese melts.
7. Repeat steps 5 and 6 to cook remaining pepper halves.
8. To serve, place each pepper half on a plate and top with ¼ cup warm salsa.

Nutrition Info: Calories per serving: 346; Carbohydrates: 14.8g; Protein: 32.6g; Fat: 19.3g; Sugar: 3.2g; Sodium: 616mg; Fiber: 1.8g

Apricot Glazed Chicken Thighs

Servings: 4

Cooking Time: 22 Minutes

Ingredients:
- 4 bone-in chicken thighs (about 2 pounds)
- olive oil
- 1 teaspoon salt
- ¼ teaspoon freshly ground black pepper
- ½ teaspoon onion powder
- ¾ cup sugar-free apricot preserves
- 1½ tablespoons Dijon mustard
- ½ teaspoon dried thyme
- 1 teaspoon low-sodium soy sauce
- fresh thyme leaves, for garnish

Directions:

1. Preheat the air fryer to 380°F.
2. Brush or spray both the air fryer basket and the chicken with the olive oil. Combine the salt, pepper and onion powder and season both sides of the chicken with the spice mixture.
3. Place the seasoned chicken thighs, skin side down in the air fryer basket. Air-fry for 10 minutes.
4. While chicken is cooking, make the glaze by combining the apricot preserves, Dijon mustard, thyme and soy sauce in a small bowl.
5. When the time is up on the air fryer, spoon half of the apricot glaze over the chicken thighs and air-fry for 2 minutes. Then flip the chicken thighs over so that the skin side is facing up and air-fry for an additional 8 minutes. Finally, spoon and spread the rest of the glaze evenly over the chicken thighs and air-fry for a final 2 minutes. Transfer the chicken to a serving platter and sprinkle the fresh thyme leaves on top.

Nutrition Info: Calories per serving: 518; Carbohydrates: 14.6g; Protein: 40.5g; Fat: 34.4g; Sugar: 0.2g; Sodium: 840mg; Fiber: 0.3g

Quick Chicken For Filling

Servings: 2

Cooking Time: 8 Minutes

Ingredients:
- 1 pound chicken tenders, skinless and boneless
- ½ teaspoon ground cumin
- ½ teaspoon garlic powder
- cooking spray

Directions:
1. Sprinkle raw chicken tenders with seasonings.
2. Spray air fryer basket lightly with cooking spray to prevent sticking.
3. Place chicken in air fryer basket in single layer.
4. Cook at 390°F for 4minutes, turn chicken strips over, and cook for an additional 4minutes.
5. Test for doneness. Thick tenders may require an additional minute or two.

Nutrition Info: Calories per serving: 435; Carbohydrates: 0.7g; Protein: 65.8g; Fat: 16.9g; Sugar: 0.2g; Sodium: 196mg; Fiber: 0.1g

Peanut Butter-barbeque Chicken

Servings: 4
Cooking Time: 20 Minutes

Ingredients:
- 1 pound boneless, skinless chicken thighs
- salt and pepper
- 1 large orange
- ½ cup sugar-free barbeque sauce
- 2 tablespoons smooth peanut butter
- 2 tablespoons chopped peanuts for garnish (optional)
- cooking spray

Directions:
1. Season chicken with salt and pepper to taste. Place in a shallow dish or plastic bag.
2. Grate orange peel, squeeze orange and reserve 1 tablespoon of juice for the sauce.
3. Pour remaining juice over chicken and marinate for 30minutes.
4. Mix together the reserved 1 tablespoon of orange juice, barbeque sauce, peanut butter, and 1 teaspoon grated orange peel.
5. Place ¼ cup of sauce mixture in a small bowl for basting. Set remaining sauce aside to serve with cooked chicken.
6. Preheat air fryer to 360°F. Spray basket with nonstick cooking spray.
7. Remove chicken from marinade, letting excess drip off. Place in air fryer basket and cook for 5minutes. Turn chicken over and cook 5minutes longer.
8. Brush both sides of chicken lightly with sauce.
9. Cook chicken 5minutes, then turn thighs one more time, again brushing both sides lightly with sauce. Cook for 5 more minutes or until chicken is done and juices run clear.
10. Serve chicken with remaining sauce on the side and garnish with chopped peanuts if you like.

Nutrition Info: Calories per serving: 316; Carbohydrates: 9g; Protein: 36.4g; Fat: 14.9g; Sugar: 5; Sodium: 174mg; Fiber: 2g

Italian Roasted Chicken Thighs

Servings: 6
Cooking Time: 14 Minutes

Ingredients:
- 6 boneless chicken thighs
- ½ teaspoon dried oregano
- ½ teaspoon garlic powder
- ½ teaspoon sea salt
- ½ teaspoon black pepper
- ¼ teaspoon crushed red pepper flakes

Directions:
1. Pat the chicken thighs with paper towel.
2. In a small bowl, mix the oregano, garlic powder, salt, pepper, and crushed red pepper flakes. Rub the spice mixture onto the chicken thighs.
3. Preheat the air fryer to 400°F.
4. Place the chicken thighs in the air fryer basket and spray with cooking spray. Cook for 10 minutes, turn over, and cook another 4 minutes. When cooking completes, the internal temperature should read 165°F.

Nutrition Info: Calories per serving: 303; Carbohydrates: 0.4g; Protein: 25.2g; Fat: 21.4g; Sugar: 0.1g; Sodium: 263mg; Fiber: 0.2g

Tandoori Chicken Legs

Servings: 2
Cooking Time: 30 Minutes

Ingredients:
- 1 cup plain yogurt
- 2 cloves garlic, minced
- 1 tablespoon grated fresh ginger
- 2 teaspoons paprika
- 2 teaspoons ground coriander
- 1 teaspoon ground turmeric
- 1 teaspoon salt
- ¼ teaspoon ground cayenne pepper
- juice of 1 lime
- 2 bone-in, skin-on chicken legs
- fresh cilantro leaves

Directions:
1. Make the marinade by combining the yogurt, garlic, ginger, spices and lime juice. Make slashes into the chicken legs to help the marinade penetrate the meat. Pour the marinade over the chicken legs, cover and let the chicken marinate for at least an hour or overnight in the refrigerator.
2. Preheat the air fryer to 380°F.
3. Transfer the chicken legs from the marinade to the air fryer basket, reserving any extra marinade. Air-fry for 15 minutes. Flip the chicken over and pour the remaining marinade over the top. Air-fry for another 15 minutes, watching to make sure it doesn't brown too much. If it does start to get too brown, you can loosely tent the chicken with aluminum foil, tucking the ends of the foil under the chicken to stop it from blowing around.
4. Serve over rice with some fresh cilantro on top.

Nutrition Info: Calories per serving: 541; Carbohydrates: 11.5g; Protein: 71g; Fat: 21.9g; Sugar: 4g; Sodium: 734mg; Fiber: 1.5g

Lemon Sage Roast Chicken

Servings: 4
Cooking Time: 60 Minutes

Ingredients:
- 1 (4-pound) chicken
- 1 bunch sage, divided
- 1 lemon, zest and juice
- salt and freshly ground black pepper

Directions:

1. Preheat the air fryer to 350°F and pour a little water into the bottom of the air fryer drawer. (This will help prevent the grease that drips into the bottom drawer from burning and smoking.)
2. Run your fingers between the skin and flesh of the chicken breasts and thighs. Push a couple of sage leaves up underneath the skin of the chicken on each breast and each thigh.
3. Push some of the lemon zest up under the skin of the chicken next to the sage. Sprinkle some of the zest inside the chicken cavity, and reserve any leftover zest. Squeeze the lemon juice all over the chicken and in the cavity as well.
4. Season the chicken, inside and out, with the salt and freshly ground black pepper. Set a few sage leaves aside for the final garnish. Crumple up the remaining sage leaves and push them into the cavity of the chicken, along with one of the squeezed lemon halves.
5. Place the chicken breast side up into the air fryer basket and air-fry for 20 minutes at 350°F. Flip the chicken over so that it is breast side down and continue to air-fry for another 20 minutes. Return the chicken to breast side up and finish air-frying for 20 more minutes. The internal temperature of the chicken should register 165°F in the thickest part of the thigh when fully cooked. Remove the chicken from the air fryer and let it rest on a cutting board for at least 5 minutes.
6. Cut the rested chicken into pieces, sprinkle with the reserved lemon zest and garnish with the reserved sage leaves.

Nutrition Info: Calories per serving: 855; Carbohydrates: 0.8g; Protein: 85.2g; Fat: 56.9g; Sugar: 0.2g; Sodium: 364mg; Fiber: 0.4g

Chicken Adobo

Servings: 6
Cooking Time: 12 Minutes

Ingredients:
- 6 boneless chicken thighs
- ¼ cup low-sodium soy sauce or tamari
- ½ cup red wine vinegar
- 4 cloves garlic, minced
- ⅛ teaspoon crushed red pepper flakes
- ½ teaspoon black pepper

Directions:
1. Place the chicken thighs into a resealable plastic bag with the soy sauce or tamari, the rice wine vinegar, the garlic, and the crushed red pepper flakes. Seal the bag and let the chicken marinate at least 1 hour in the refrigerator.
2. Preheat the air fryer to 400°F.
3. Drain the chicken and pat dry with a paper towel. Season the chicken with black pepper and liberally spray with cooking spray.
4. Place the chicken in the air fryer basket and cook for 9 minutes, turn over at 9 minutes and check for an internal temperature of 165°F, and cook another 3 minutes.

Nutrition Info: Calories per serving: 314; Carbohydrates: 1.8g; Protein: 25.9g; Fat: 21.3g; Sugar: 0.3g; Sodium: 707mg; Fiber: 0.2g

VEGETABLE SIDE DISHES RECIPES

Perfect Broccoli

Servings: 4
Cooking Time: 12 Minutes

Ingredients:

- 5 cups (about 1 pound 10 ounces) 1- to 1½-inch fresh broccoli florets (not frozen)
- Olive oil spray
- ¾ teaspoon Table salt

Directions:

1. Preheat the air fryer to 375°F.
2. Put the broccoli florets in a big bowl, coat them generously with olive oil spray, then toss to coat all surfaces, even down into the crannies, spraying them in a couple of times more. Sprinkle the salt on top and toss again.
3. When the machine is at temperature, pour the florets into the basket. Air-fry for 10 minutes, tossing and rearranging the pieces twice so that all the covered or touching bits are eventually exposed to the air currents, until lightly browned but still crunchy. (If the machine is at 360°F, you may have to add 2 minutes to the cooking time.)
4. Pour the florets into a serving bowl. Cool for a minute or two, then serve hot.

Nutrition Info: Calories per serving: 39; Carbohydrates: 7.6g; Protein: 3.2g; Fat: 13.1g; Sugar: 1.9g; Sodium: 474mg; Fiber: 3g

Roasted Cauliflower With Garlic And Capers

Servings: 3
Cooking Time: 10 Minutes

Ingredients:
- 3 cups (about 15 ounces) 1-inch cauliflower florets
- 2 tablespoons Olive oil
- 1½ tablespoons Drained and rinsed capers, chopped
- 2 teaspoons Minced garlic
- ¼ teaspoon Table salt
- Up to ¼ teaspoon Red pepper flakes

Directions:
1. Preheat the air fryer to 375°F.
2. Stir the cauliflower florets, olive oil, capers, garlic, salt, and red pepper flakes in a large bowl until the florets are evenly coated.
3. When the machine is at temperature, put the florets in the basket, spreading them out to as close to one layer as you can. Air-fry for 10 minutes, tossing once to get any covered pieces exposed to the air currents, until tender and lightly browned.
4. Dump the contents of the basket into a serving bowl or onto a serving platter. Cool for a minute or two before serving.

Nutrition Info: Calories per serving: 109; Carbohydrates: 6.2g; Protein: 2.2g; Fat: 9.5g; Sugar: 2.5g; Sodium: 352mg; Fiber: 2.7g

Perfect Broccolini

Servings: 4

Cooking Time: 15 Minutes

Ingredients:
- 1 pound Broccolini
- Olive oil spray
- Coarse sea salt or kosher salt

Directions:
1. Preheat the air fryer to 375°F.
2. Place the broccolini on a cutting board. Generously coat it with olive oil spray, turning the vegetables and rearranging them before spraying a couple of times more, to make sure everything's well coated, even the flowery bits in their heads.
3. When the machine is at temperature, pile the broccolini in the basket, spreading it into as close to one layer as you can. Air-fry for 5 minutes, tossing once to get any covered or touching parts exposed to the air currents, until the leaves begin to get brown and even crisp. Watch carefully and use this visual cue to know the moment to stop the cooking.
4. Transfer the broccolini to a platter. Spread out the pieces and sprinkle them with salt to taste.

Nutrition Info: Calories per serving: 39; Carbohydrates: 7.5g; Protein: 3.2g; Fat: 0.4g; Sugar: 1.9g; Sodium: 76mg; Fiber: 3g

Tandoori Cauliflower

Servings: 4
Cooking Time: 10 Minutes

Ingredients:
- ½ cup Plain full-fat yogurt (not Greek yogurt)
- 1½ teaspoons Yellow curry powder, purchased or homemade (see the headnote)
- 1½ teaspoons Lemon juice
- ¾ teaspoon Table salt (optional)
- 4½ cups (about 1 pound 2 ounces) 2-inch cauliflower florets

Directions:
1. Preheat the air fryer to 400°F.
2. Whisk the yogurt, curry powder, lemon juice, and salt (if using) in a large bowl until uniform. Add the florets and stir gently to coat the florets well and evenly. Even better, use your clean, dry hands to get the yogurt mixture down into all the nooks of the florets.
3. When the machine is at temperature, transfer the florets to the basket, spreading them gently into as close to one layer as you can. Air-fry for 10 minutes, tossing and rearranging the florets twice so that any covered or touching parts are exposed to the air currents, until lightly browned and tender if still a bit crunchy.
4. Pour the contents of the basket onto a wire rack. Cool for at least 5 minutes before serving, or serve at room temperature.

Nutrition Info: Calories per serving: 53; Carbohydrates: 8.6g; Protein: 4.1g; Fat: 0.6g; Sugar: 4g; Sodium: 494mg; Fiber: 3.1g

Tomato Candy

Servings: 12
Cooking Time: 120 Minutes

Ingredients:
- 6 Small Roma or plum tomatoes, halved lengthwise
- 1½ teaspoons Coarse sea salt or kosher salt

Directions:
1. Before you turn the machine on, set the tomatoes cut side up in a single layer in the basket (or the basket attachment). They can touch each other, but try to leave at least a fraction of an inch between them (depending, of course, on the size of the basket or basket attachment). Sprinkle the cut sides of the tomatoes with the salt.
2. Set the machine to cook at 225°F (or 230°F, if that's the closest setting). Put the basket in the machine and air-fry for 2 hours, or until the tomatoes are dry but pliable, with a little moisture down in their centers.
3. Remove the basket from the machine and cool the tomatoes in it for 10 minutes before gently transferring them to a plate for serving, or to a shallow dish that you can cover and store in the refrigerator for up to 1 week.

Nutrition Info: Calories per serving: 8; Carbohydrates: 1.8g; Protein: 0.4g; Fat: 0.1g; Sugar: 1.2g; Sodium: 293mg; Fiber: 0.6g

Roasted Garlic And Thyme Tomatoes

Servings: 2
Cooking Time: 15 Minutes

Ingredients:
- 4 Roma tomatoes
- 1 tablespoon olive oil
- salt and freshly ground black pepper
- 1 clove garlic, minced
- ½ teaspoon dried thyme

Directions:
1. Preheat the air fryer to 390°F.
2. Cut the tomatoes in half and scoop out the seeds and any pithy parts with your fingers. Place the tomatoes in a bowl and toss with the olive oil, salt, pepper, garlic and thyme.
3. Transfer the tomatoes to the air fryer, cut side up. Air-fry for 15 minutes. The edges should just start to brown. Let the tomatoes cool to an edible temperature for a few minutes and then use in pastas, on top of crostini, or as an accompaniment to any poultry, meat or fish.

Nutrition Info: Calories per serving: 107; Carbohydrates: 10.2g; Protein: 2.3g; Fat: 7.5g; Sugar: 4g; Sodium: 90mg; Fiber: 3.1g

Simple Roasted Sweet Potatoes

Servings: 4
Cooking Time: 45 Minutes

Ingredients:
- 2 10- to 12-ounce sweet potato(es)

Directions:
1. Preheat the air fryer to 350°F.
2. Prick the sweet potato(es) in four or five different places with the tines of a flatware fork (not in a line but all around).
3. When the machine is at temperature, set the sweet potato(es) in the basket with as much air space between them as possible. Air-fry undisturbed for 45 minutes, or until soft when pricked with a fork.
4. Use kitchen tongs to transfer the sweet potato(es) to a wire rack. Cool for 5 minutes before serving.

Nutrition Info: Calories per serving: 128; Carbohydrates: 20.6g; Protein: 2.9g; Fat: 13.1g; Sugar: 7g; Sodium: 51mg; Fiber: 4.7g

Cauliflower

Servings: 4
Cooking Time: 6 Minutes

Ingredients:
- ½ cup water
- 1 10-ounce package frozen cauliflower (florets)
- 1 teaspoon lemon pepper seasoning

Directions:
1. Pour the water into air fryer drawer.
2. Pour the frozen cauliflower into the air fryer basket and sprinkle with lemon pepper seasoning.
3. Cook at 390°F for approximately 6 minutes.

Nutrition Info: Calories per serving: 19; Carbohydrates: 4.1g; Protein: 1.5g; Fat: 0.1g; Sugar: 1.7g; Sodium: 22mg; Fiber: 1.9g

Shoestring Butternut Squash Fries

Servings: 3

Cooking Time: 16 Minutes

Ingredients:
- 1 pound 2 ounces Spiralized butternut squash strands
- Vegetable oil spray
- To taste Coarse sea salt or kosher salt

Directions:
1. Preheat the air fryer to 375°F.
2. Place the spiralized squash in a big bowl. Coat the strands with vegetable oil spray, toss well, coat again, and toss several times to make sure all the strands have been oiled.
3. When the machine is at temperature, pour the strands into the basket and spread them out into as even a layer as possible. Air-fry for 16 minutes, tossing and rearranging the strands every 4 minutes, or until they're lightly browned and crisp.
4. Pour the contents of the basket into a serving bowl, add salt to taste, and toss well before serving hot.

Nutrition Info: Calories per serving: 68; Carbohydrates: 15.6g; Protein: 2.2g; Fat: 0.2g; Sugar: 3.3g; Sodium: 56mg; Fiber: 3g

Charred Radicchio Salad

Servings: 4

Cooking Time: 5 Minutes

Ingredients:
- 2 Small 5- to 6-ounce radicchio head(s)
- 3 tablespoons Olive oil
- ½ teaspoon Table salt
- 2 tablespoons Balsamic vinegar
- Up to ¼ teaspoon Red pepper flakes

Directions:
1. Preheat the air fryer to 375°F.
2. Cut the radicchio head(s) into quarters through the stem end. Brush the oil over the heads, particularly getting it between the leaves along the cut sides. Sprinkle the radicchio quarters with the salt.
3. When the machine is at temperature, set the quarters cut sides up in the basket with as much air space between them as possible. They should not touch. Air-fry undisturbed for 5 minutes, watching carefully because they burn quickly, until blackened in bits and soft.
4. Use a nonstick-safe spatula to transfer the quarters to a cutting board. Cool for a minute or two, then cut out the thick stems inside the heads. Discard these tough bits and chop the remaining heads into bite-size bits. Scrape them into a bowl. Add the vinegar and red pepper flakes. Toss well and serve warm.

Nutrition Info: Calories per serving: 108; Carbohydrates: 3.3g; Protein: 1g; Fat: 10.7g; Sugar: 0.5g; Sodium: 307mg; Fiber: 0.7g

Roasted Peppers With Balsamic Vinegar And Basil

Servings: 6

Cooking Time: 12 Minutes

Ingredients:
- 4 Small or medium red or yellow bell peppers
- 3 tablespoons Olive oil
- 1 tablespoon Balsamic vinegar
- Up to 6 Fresh basil leaves, torn up

Directions:
1. Preheat the air fryer to 400°F.
2. When the machine is at temperature, put the peppers in the basket with at least ¼ inch between them. Air-fry undisturbed for 12 minutes, until blistered, even blackened in places.
3. Use kitchen tongs to transfer the peppers to a medium bowl. Cover the bowl with plastic wrap. Set aside at room temperature for 30 minutes.
4. Uncover the bowl and use kitchen tongs to transfer the peppers to a cutting board or work surface. Peel off the filmy exterior skin. If there are blackened bits under it, these can stay on the peppers. Cut off and remove the stem ends. Split open the peppers and discard any seeds and their spongy membranes. Slice the peppers into ½-inch- to 1-inch-wide strips.
5. Put these in a clean bowl and gently toss them with the oil, vinegar, and basil. Serve at once. Or cover and store at room temperature for up to 4 hours or in the refrigerator for up to 5 days.

Nutrition Info: Calories per serving: 86; Carbohydrates: 6g; Protein: 0.8g; Fat: 13.1g; Sugar: 4g; Sodium: 4mg; Fiber: 1.1g

Sweet Potato Curly Fries

Servings: 4
Cooking Time: 10 Minutes

Ingredients:
- 2 medium sweet potatoes, washed
- 2 tablespoons avocado oil
- ¾ teaspoon salt, divided
- 1 medium avocado
- ½ teaspoon garlic powder
- ½ teaspoon paprika
- ¼ teaspoon black pepper
- ½ juice lime
- 3 tablespoons fresh cilantro

Directions:
1. Preheat the air fryer to 400°F.
2. Using a spiralizer, create curly spirals with the sweet potatoes. Keep the pieces about 1½ inches long. Continue until all the potatoes are used.
3. In a large bowl, toss the curly sweet potatoes with the avocado oil and ½ teaspoon of the salt.
4. Place the potatoes in the air fryer basket and cook for 5 minutes; shake and cook another 5 minutes.
5. While cooking, add the avocado, garlic, paprika, pepper, the remaining ¼ teaspoon of salt, lime juice, and cilantro to a blender and process until smooth. Set aside.
6. When cooking completes, remove the fries and serve warm with the lime avocado sauce.

Nutrition Info: Calories per serving: 142; Carbohydrates: 19.6g; Protein: 1.9g; Fat: 5.4g; Sugar: 0.6g; Sodium: 447mg; Fiber: 5g

Roasted Yellow Squash And Onions

Servings: 3

Cooking Time: 20 Minutes

Ingredients:
- 1 medium (8-inch) squash Yellow or summer crookneck squash, cut into ½-inch-thick rounds
- 1½ cups (1 large onion) Yellow or white onion, roughly chopped
- ¾ teaspoon Table salt
- ¼ teaspoon Ground cumin (optional)
- Olive oil spray
- 1½ tablespoons Lemon or lime juice

Directions:
1. Preheat the air fryer to 375°F.
2. Toss the squash rounds, onion, salt, and cumin (if using) in a large bowl. Lightly coat the vegetables with olive oil spray, toss again, spray again, and keep at it until the vegetables are evenly coated.
3. When the machine is at temperature, scrape the contents of the bowl into the basket, spreading the vegetables out into as close to one layer as you can. Air-fry for 20 minutes, tossing once very gently, until the squash and onions are soft, even a little browned at the edges.
4. Pour the contents of the basket into a serving bowl, add the lemon or lime juice, and toss gently but well to coat. Serve warm or at room temperature.

Nutrition Info: Calories per serving: 36; Carbohydrates: 7.8g; Protein: 1.5g; Fat: 0.3g; Sugar: 3.7g; Sodium: 584mg; Fiber: 2g

Crispy Brussels Sprouts

Servings: 3
Cooking Time: 12 Minutes

Ingredients:
- 1¼ pounds Medium, 2-inch-in-length Brussels sprouts
- 1½ tablespoons Olive oil
- ¾ teaspoon Table salt

Directions:
1. Preheat the air fryer to 400°F.
2. Halve each Brussels sprout through the stem end, pulling off and discarding any discolored outer leaves. Put the sprout halves in a large bowl, add the oil and salt, and stir well to coat evenly, until the Brussels sprouts are glistening.
3. When the machine is at temperature, scrape the contents of the bowl into the basket, gently spreading the Brussels sprout halves into as close to one layer as possible. Air-fry for 12 minutes, gently tossing and rearranging the vegetables twice to get all covered or touching parts exposed to the air currents, until crisp and browned at the edges.
4. Gently pour the contents of the basket onto a wire rack. Cool for a minute or two before serving.

Nutrition Info: Calories per serving: 142; Carbohydrates: 14.6g; Protein: 6.4g; Fat: 7.6g; Sugar: 4.1g; Sodium: 629mg; Fiber: 3.1g

Blistered Tomatoes

Servings: 20
Cooking Time: 15 Minutes

Ingredients:
- 1½ pounds Cherry or grape tomatoes
- Olive oil spray
- 1½ teaspoons Balsamic vinegar
- ¼ teaspoon Table salt
- ¼ teaspoon Ground black pepper

Directions:
1. Put the basket in a drawer-style air fryer, or a baking tray in the lower third of a toaster oven–style air fryer. Place a 6-inch round cake pan in the basket or on the tray for a small batch, a 7-inch round cake pan for a medium batch, or an 8-inch round cake pan for a large one. Heat the air fryer to 400°F with the pan in the basket. When the machine is at temperature, keep heating the pan for 5 minutes more.
2. Place the tomatoes in a large bowl, coat them with the olive oil spray, toss gently, then spritz a couple of times more, tossing after each spritz, until the tomatoes are glistening.
3. Pour the tomatoes into the cake pan and air-fry undisturbed for 10 minutes, or until they split and begin to brown.
4. Use kitchen tongs and a nonstick-safe spatula, or silicone baking mitts, to remove the cake pan from the basket. Toss the hot tomatoes with the vinegar, salt, and pepper. Cool in the pan for a few minutes before serving.

Nutrition Info: Calories per serving: 6; Carbohydrates: 1.3g; Protein: 2.2g; Fat: 0.1g; Sugar: 0.9g; Sodium: 33mg; Fiber: 0.4g

Fried Cauliflower With Parmesan Lemon Dressing

Servings: 4
Cooking Time: 12 Minutes

Ingredients:
- 4 cups cauliflower florets (about half a large head)
- 1 tablespoon olive oil
- salt and freshly ground black pepper
- 1 teaspoon finely chopped lemon zest
- 1 tablespoon fresh lemon juice (about half a lemon)
- ¼ cup grated Parmigiano-Reggiano cheese
- 4 tablespoons extra virgin olive oil
- ¼ teaspoon salt
- lots of freshly ground black pepper
- 1 tablespoon chopped fresh parsley

Directions:
1. Preheat the air fryer to 400°F.
2. Toss the cauliflower florets with the olive oil, salt and freshly ground black pepper. Air-fry for 12 minutes, shaking the basket a couple of times during the cooking process.
3. While the cauliflower is frying, make the dressing. Combine the lemon zest, lemon juice, Parmigiano-Reggiano cheese and olive oil in a small bowl. Season with salt and lots of freshly ground black pepper. Stir in the parsley.
4. Turn the fried cauliflower out onto a serving platter and drizzle the dressing over the top.

Nutrition Info: Calories per serving: 197; Carbohydrates: 5.5g; Protein: 4.1g; Fat: 19.1g; Sugar: 2.5g; Sodium: 209mg; Fiber: 2.6g

Roman Artichokes

Servings: 4
Cooking Time: 12 Minutes

Ingredients:
- 2 9-ounce box(es) frozen artichoke heart quarters, thawed
- 1½ tablespoons Olive oil
- 2 teaspoons Minced garlic
- 1 teaspoon Table salt
- Up to ½ teaspoon Red pepper flakes

Directions:
1. Preheat the air fryer to 400°F.
2. Gently toss the artichoke heart quarters, oil, garlic, salt, and red pepper flakes in a bowl until the quarters are well coated.
3. When the machine is at temperature, scrape the contents of the bowl into the basket. Spread the artichoke heart quarters out into as close to one layer as possible. Air-fry undisturbed for 8 minutes. Gently toss and rearrange the quarters so that any covered or touching parts are now exposed to the air currents, then air-fry undisturbed for 4 minutes more, until very crisp.
4. Gently pour the contents of the basket onto a wire rack. Cool for a few minutes before serving.

Nutrition Info: Calories per serving: 108; Carbohydrates: 14g; Protein: 4.3g; Fat: 5.5g; Sugar: 1.3g; Sodium: 702mg; Fiber: 7g

Onions

Servings: 4
Cooking Time: 18 Minutes

Ingredients:
- 2 yellow onions (Vidalia or 1015 recommended)
- salt and pepper
- ¼ teaspoon ground thyme
- ¼ teaspoon smoked paprika
- 2 teaspoons olive oil
- 1 ounce Gruyère cheese, grated

Directions:
1. Peel onions and halve lengthwise (vertically).
2. Sprinkle cut sides of onions with salt, pepper, thyme, and paprika.
3. Place each onion half, cut-surface up, on a large square of aluminum foil. Pull sides of foil up to cup around onion. Drizzle cut surface of onions with oil.
4. Crimp foil at top to seal closed.
5. Place wrapped onions in air fryer basket and cook at 390°F for 18 minutes. When done, onions should be soft enough to pierce with fork but still slightly firm.
6. Open foil just enough to sprinkle each onion with grated cheese.
7. Cook for 30 seconds to 1 minute to melt cheese.

Nutrition Info: Calories per serving: 72; Carbohydrates: 5.3g; Protein: 2.8g; Fat: 4.7g; Sugar: 2.4g; Sodium: 29mg; Fiber: 1.3g

Mushrooms, Sautéed

Servings: 2

Cooking Time: 4 Minutes

Ingredients:
- 8 ounces sliced white mushrooms, rinsed and well drained
- ¼ teaspoon garlic powder
- 1 tablespoon Worcestershire sauce

Directions:
1. Place mushrooms in a large bowl and sprinkle with garlic powder and Worcestershire. Stir well to distribute seasonings evenly.
2. Place in air fryer basket and cook at 390°F for 4 minutes, until tender.

Nutrition Info: Calories per serving: 33; Carbohydrates: 5.5g; Protein: 3.6g; Fat: 13.1g; Sugar: 3.5g; Sodium: 89mg; Fiber: 1.2g

APPETIZERS AND SNACKS

Carrot Chips

Servings: 4

Cooking Time: 10 Minutes

Ingredients:
- 1 pound carrots, thinly sliced
- 2 tablespoons extra-virgin olive oil
- ¼ teaspoon garlic powder
- ¼ teaspoon black pepper
- ½ teaspoon salt

Directions:
1. Preheat the air fryer to 390°F.
2. In a medium bowl, toss the carrot slices with the olive oil, garlic powder, pepper, and salt.
3. Liberally spray the air fryer basket with olive oil mist.
4. Place the carrot slices in the air fryer basket. To allow for even cooking, don't overlap the carrots; cook in batches if necessary.
5. Cook for 5 minutes, shake the basket, and cook another 5 minutes.
6. Remove from the basket and serve warm. Repeat with the remaining carrot slices until they're all cooked.

Nutrition Info: Calories per serving: 107; Carbohydrates: 11g; Protein: 2.2g; Fat: 7g; Sugar: 5g; Sodium: 369mg; Fiber: 2.4g

Okra Chips

Servings: 4
Cooking Time: 16 Minutes

Ingredients:
- 1¼ pounds Thin fresh okra pods, cut into 1-inch pieces
- 1½ tablespoons Vegetable or canola oil
- ¾ teaspoon Coarse sea salt or kosher salt

Directions:
1. Preheat the air fryer to 400°F.
2. Toss the okra, oil, and salt in a large bowl until the pieces are well and evenly coated.
3. When the machine is at temperature, pour the contents of the bowl into the basket. Air-fry, tossing several times, for 16 minutes, or until crisp and quite brown (maybe even a little blackened on the thin bits).
4. Pour the contents of the basket onto a wire rack. Cool for a couple of minutes before serving.

Nutrition Info: Calories per serving: 103; Carbohydrates: 10.6g; Protein: 2.7g; Fat: 5.5g; Sugar: 2g; Sodium: 448mg; Fiber: 4g

Crispy Spiced Chickpeas

Servings: 4
Cooking Time: 20 Minutes

Ingredients:

- 1 (15-ounce) can chickpeas, drained (or 1½ cups cooked chickpeas)
- ½ teaspoon salt
- ½ teaspoon chili powder
- ¼ teaspoon ground cinnamon
- ⅛ teaspoon smoked paprika
- pinch ground cayenne pepper
- 1 tablespoon olive oil

Directions:

1. Preheat the air fryer to 400°F.
2. Dry the chickpeas as well as you can with a clean kitchen towel, rubbing off any loose skins as necessary. Combine the spices in a small bowl. Toss the chickpeas with the olive oil and then add the spices and toss again.
3. Air-fry for 15 minutes, shaking the basket a couple of times while they cook.
4. Check the chickpeas to see if they are crispy enough and if necessary, air-fry for another 5 minutes to crisp them further. Serve warm, or cool to room temperature and store in an airtight container for up to two weeks.

Nutrition Info: Calories per serving: 158; Carbohydrates: 19.6g; Protein: 5.3g; Fat: 4.8g; Sugar: 0g; Sodium: 612mg; Fiber: 3.8g

Warm And Salty Edamame

Servings: 4
Cooking Time: 10 Minutes

Ingredients:
- 1 pound Unshelled edamame
- Vegetable oil spray
- ¾ teaspoon Coarse sea salt or kosher salt

Directions:
1. Preheat the air fryer to 400°F.
2. Place the edamame in a large bowl and lightly coat them with vegetable oil spray. Toss well, spray again, and toss until they are evenly coated.
3. When the machine is at temperature, pour the edamame into the basket and air-fry, tossing the basket quite often to rearrange the edamame, for 7 minutes, or until warm and aromatic. (Air-fry for 10 minutes if the edamame were frozen and not thawed.)
4. Pour the edamame into a bowl and sprinkle the salt on top. Toss well, then set aside for a couple of minutes before serving with an empty bowl on the side for the pods.

Nutrition Info: Calories per serving: 167; Carbohydrates: 12.5g; Protein: 14.7g; Fat: 7.7g; Sugar: 0g; Sodium: 377mg; Fiber: 4.8g

Kale Chips

Servings: 2
Cooking Time: 5 Minutes

Ingredients:
- 4 Medium kale leaves, about 1 ounce each
- 2 teaspoons Olive oil
- 2 teaspoons Regular or low-sodium soy sauce or gluten-free tamari sauce

Directions:
1. Preheat the air fryer to 400°F.
2. Cut the stems from the leaves (all the stems, all the way up the leaf). Tear each leaf into three pieces. Put them in a large bowl.
3. Add the olive oil and soy or tamari sauce. Toss well to coat. You can even gently rub the leaves along the side of the bowl to get the liquids to stick to them.
4. When the machine is at temperature, put the leaf pieces in the basket in one layer. Air-fry for 5 minutes, turning and rearranging with kitchen tongs once halfway through, until the chips are dried out and crunchy. Watch carefully so they don't turn dark brown at the edges.
5. Gently pour the contents of the basket onto a wire rack. Cool for at least 5 minutes before serving. The chips can keep for up to 8 hours uncovered on the rack (provided it's not a humid day).

Nutrition Info: Calories per serving: 70; Carbohydrates: 6.3g; Protein: 2g; Fat: 4.7g; Sugar: 0.3g; Sodium: 318mg; Fiber: 0.9g

Halloumi Fries

Servings: 4
Cooking Time: 12 Minutes

Ingredients:
- 1½ tablespoons Olive oil
- 1½ teaspoons Minced garlic
- ⅛ teaspoon Dried oregano
- ⅛ teaspoon Dried thyme
- ⅛ teaspoon Table salt
- ⅛ teaspoon Ground black pepper
- ¾ pound Halloumi

Directions:
1. Preheat the air fryer to 400°F.
2. Whisk the oil, garlic, oregano, thyme, salt, and pepper in a medium bowl.
3. Lay the piece of halloumi flat on a cutting board. Slice it widthwise into ½-inch-thick sticks. Cut each stick lengthwise into ½-inch-thick batons.
4. Put these batons into the olive oil mixture. Toss gently but well to coat.
5. Place the batons in the basket in a single layer. Air-fry undisturbed for 12 minutes, or until lightly browned, particularly at the edges.
6. Dump the fries out onto a wire rack. They may need a little coaxing with a nonstick-safe spatula to come free. Cool for a couple of minutes before serving hot.

Nutrition Info: Calories per serving: 355; Carbohydrates: 2.2g; Protein: 18.4g; Fat: 30.4g; Sugar: 2g; Sodium: 438mg; Fiber: 0g

Cinnamon Apple Crisps

Servings: 2
Cooking Time: 22 Minutes

Ingredients:
- 1 large apple
- ½ teaspoon ground cinnamon
- 2 teaspoons avocado oil or coconut oil

Directions:
1. Preheat the air fryer to 300°F.
2. Using a mandolin or knife, slice the apples to ¼-inch thickness. Pat the apples dry with a paper towel or kitchen cloth. Sprinkle the apple slices with ground cinnamon. Spray or drizzle the oil over the top of the apple slices and toss to coat.
3. Place the apple slices in the air fryer basket. To allow for even cooking, don't overlap the slices; cook in batches if necessary.
4. Cook for 20 minutes, shaking the basket every 5 minutes. After 20 minutes, increase the air fryer temperature to 330°F and cook another 2 minutes, shaking the basket every 30 seconds. Remove the apples from the basket before they get too dark.
5. Spread the chips out onto paper towels to cool completely, at least 5 minutes. Repeat with the remaining apple slices until they're all cooked.

Nutrition Info: Calories per serving: 66; Carbohydrates: 16g; Protein: 0.4g; Fat: 0.8g; Sugar: 7g; Sodium: 1mg; Fiber: 3.2g

Crispy Tofu Bites

Servings: 4
Cooking Time: 20 Minutes

Ingredients:
- 1 pound Extra firm unflavored tofu
- Vegetable oil spray

Directions:
1. Wrap the piece of tofu in a triple layer of paper towels. Place it on a wooden cutting board and set a large pot on top of it to press out excess moisture. Set aside for 10 minutes.
2. Preheat the air fryer to 400°F.
3. Remove the pot and unwrap the tofu. Cut it into 1-inch cubes. Place these in a bowl and coat them generously with vegetable oil spray. Toss gently, then spray generously again before tossing, until all are glistening.
4. Gently pour the tofu pieces into the basket, spread them into as close to one layer as possible, and air-fry for 20 minutes, using kitchen tongs to gently rearrange the pieces at the 7- and 14-minute marks, until light brown and crisp.
5. Gently pour the tofu pieces onto a wire rack. Cool for 5 minutes before serving warm.

Nutrition Info: Calories per serving: 79; Carbohydrates: 1.9g; Protein: 9.3g; Fat: 4.7g; Sugar: 0.7g; Sodium: 14mg; Fiber: 1g

Zucchini Chips

Servings: 3
Cooking Time: 17 Minutes

Ingredients:
- 1½ small (about 1½ cups) Zucchini, washed but not peeled, and cut into ¼-inch-thick rounds
- Olive oil spray
- ¼ teaspoon Table salt

Directions:
1. Preheat the air fryer to 375°F.
2. Lay some paper towels on your work surface. Set the zucchini rounds on top, then set more paper towels over the rounds. Press gently to remove some of the moisture. Remove the top layer of paper towels and lightly coat the rounds with olive oil spray on both sides.
3. When the machine is at temperature, set the rounds in the basket, overlapping them a bit as needed. (They'll shrink as they cook.) Air-fry for 15 minutes, tossing and rearranging the rounds at the 5- and 10-minute marks, until browned, soft, yet crisp at the edges. (You'll need to air-fry the rounds 2 minutes more if the temperature is set at 360°F.)
4. Gently pour the contents of the basket onto a wire rack. Cool for at least 10 minutes or up to 2 hours before serving.

Nutrition Info: Calories per serving: 33; Carbohydrates: 6.9g; Protein: 2.5g; Fat: 0.4g; Sugar: 3.6g; Sodium: 215mg; Fiber: 2.3g

Chicken Shawarma Bites

Servings: 6
Cooking Time: 22 Minutes

Ingredients:
- 1½ pounds Boneless skinless chicken thighs, trimmed of any fat and cut into 1-inch pieces
- 1½ tablespoons Olive oil
- Up to 1½ tablespoons Minced garlic
- ½ teaspoon Table salt
- ¼ teaspoon Ground cardamom
- ¼ teaspoon Ground cinnamon
- ¼ teaspoon Ground cumin
- ¼ teaspoon Mild paprika
- Up to a ¼ teaspoon Grated nutmeg
- ¼ teaspoon Ground black pepper

Directions:
1. Preheat the air fryer to 400°F.
2. Mix all the ingredients in a large bowl until the chicken is thoroughly and evenly coated in the oil and spices.
3. When the machine is at temperature, scrape the coated chicken pieces into the basket and spread them out into one layer as much as you can. Air-fry for 22 minutes, shaking the basket at least three times during cooking to rearrange the pieces, until well browned and crisp.
4. Pour the chicken pieces onto a wire rack. Cool for 5 minutes before serving.

Nutrition Info: Calories per serving: 250; Carbohydrates: 1g; Protein: 33g; Fat: 12g; Sugar: 0.1g; Sodium: 292mg; Fiber: 0.2g

Garlic Parmesan Kale Chips

Servings: 6
Cooking Time: 6 Minutes

Ingredients:
- 16 large kale leaves, washed and thick stems removed
- 1 tablespoon avocado oil
- ½ teaspoon garlic powder
- 1 teaspoon low-sodium soy sauce or tamari
- ¼ cup grated Parmesan cheese

Directions:
1. Preheat the air fryer to 370°F.
2. Make a stack of kale leaves and cut them into 4 pieces.
3. Place the kale pieces into a large bowl. Drizzle the avocado oil onto the kale and rub to coat. Add the garlic powder, soy sauce or tamari, and cheese, tossing to coat.
4. Pour the chips into the air fryer basket and cook for 3 minutes, shake the basket, and cook another 3 minutes, checking for crispness every minute. When done cooking, pour the kale chips onto paper towels and cool at least 5 minutes before serving.

Nutrition Info: Calories per serving: 53; Carbohydrates: 8g; Protein: 3.7g; Fat: 1.1g; Sugar: 0.1g; Sodium: 110mg; Fiber: 1.3g

Za'atar Garbanzo Beans

Servings: 6
Cooking Time: 12 Minutes

Ingredients:
- One 14.5-ounce can garbanzo beans, drained and rinsed
- 1 tablespoon extra-virgin olive oil
- 6 teaspoons za'atar seasoning mix
- 2 tablespoons chopped parsley
- Salt and pepper, to taste

Directions:
1. Preheat the air fryer to 390°F.
2. In a medium bowl, toss the garbanzo beans with olive oil and za'atar seasoning.
3. Pour the beans into the air fryer basket and cook for 12 minutes, or until toasted as you like. Stir every 3 minutes while roasting.
4. Remove the beans from the air fryer basket into a serving bowl, top with fresh chopped parsley, and season with salt and pepper.

Nutrition Info: Calories per serving: 102; Carbohydrates: 15.6g; Protein: 3.4g; Fat: 3.1g; Sugar: 0g; Sodium: 233mg; Fiber: 3.1g

Baba Ghanouj

Servings: 2
Cooking Time: 40 Minutes

Ingredients:
- 2 Small (12-ounce) purple Italian eggplant(s)
- ¼ cup Olive oil
- ¼ cup Tahini
- ½ teaspoon Ground black pepper
- ¼ teaspoon Onion powder
- ¼ teaspoon Mild smoked paprika (optional)
- Up to 1 teaspoon Table salt

Directions:
1. Preheat the air fryer to 400°F.
2. Prick the eggplant(s) on all sides with a fork. When the machine is at temperature, set the eggplant(s) in the basket in one layer. Air-fry undisturbed for 40 minutes, or until blackened and soft.
3. Remove the basket from the machine. Cool the eggplant(s) in the basket for 20 minutes.
4. Use a nonstick-safe spatula, and perhaps a flatware tablespoon for balance, to gently transfer the eggplant(s) to a bowl. The juices will run out. Make sure the bowl is close to the basket. Split the eggplant(s) open.
5. Scrape the soft insides of half an eggplant into a food processor. Repeat with the remaining piece(s). Add any juices from the bowl to the eggplant in the food processor, but discard the skins and stems.
6. Add the olive oil, tahini, pepper, onion powder, and smoked paprika (if using). Add about half the salt, then cover and process until smooth, stopping the machine at least once to scrape down the inside of the canister. Check the spread for salt and add more as needed. Scrape the baba ghanouj into a bowl and serve warm, or set aside at room temperature for up to 2 hours, or cover and store in the refrigerator for up to 4 days.

Nutrition Info: Calories per serving: 321; Carbohydrates: 14.6g; Protein: 3.8g; Fat: 30g; Sugar: 5g; Sodium: 119mg; Fiber: 6.2g

Blistered Shishito Peppers

Servings: 3
Cooking Time: 5 Minutes

Ingredients:
- 6 ounces (about 18) Shishito peppers
- Vegetable oil spray
- For garnishing Coarse sea or kosher salt and lemon wedges

Directions:
1. Preheat the air fryer to 400°F.
2. Put the peppers in a bowl and lightly coat them with vegetable oil spray. Toss gently, spray again, and toss until the peppers are glistening but not drenched.
3. Pour the peppers into the basket, spread them into as close to one layer as you can, and air-fry for 5 minutes, tossing and rearranging the peppers at the 2- and 4-minute marks, until the peppers are blistered and even blackened in spots.
4. Pour the peppers into a bowl, add salt to taste, and toss gently. Serve the peppers with lemon wedges to squeeze over them.

Nutrition Info: Calories per serving: 19; Carbohydrates: 3.8g; Protein: 1.3g; Fat: 0g; Sugar: 2g; Sodium: 4mg; Fiber: 2.5g

Green Olive And Mushroom Tapenade

Servings: 4

Cooking Time: 10 Minutes

Ingredients:
- ¾ pound Brown or Baby Bella mushrooms, sliced
- 1½ cups (about ½ pound) Pitted green olives
- 3 tablespoons Olive oil
- 1½ tablespoons Fresh oregano leaves, loosely packed
- ¼ teaspoon Ground black pepper

Directions:
1. Preheat the air fryer to 400°F.
2. When the machine is at temperature, arrange the mushroom slices in as close to an even layer as possible in the basket. They will overlap and even stack on top of each other.
3. Air-fry for 10 minutes, tossing the basket and rearranging the mushrooms every 2 minutes, until shriveled but with still-noticeable moisture.
4. Pour the mushrooms into a food processor. Add the olives, olive oil, oregano leaves, and pepper. Cover and process until grainy, not too much, just not fully smooth for better texture, stopping the machine at least once to scrape down the inside of the canister. Scrape the tapenade into a bowl and serve warm, or cover and refrigerate for up to 4 days. (The tapenade will taste better if it comes back to room temperature before serving.)

Nutrition Info: Calories per serving: 179; Carbohydrates: 7.5g; Protein: 3.4g; Fat: 17g; Sugar: 1.5g; Sodium: 500mg; Fiber: 3.4g

Roasted Red Pepper Dip

Servings: 4

Cooking Time: 15 Minutes

Ingredients:
- 2 Medium-size red bell pepper(s)
- 1¾ cups (one 15-ounce can) Canned white beans, drained and rinsed
- 1 tablespoon Fresh oregano leaves, packed
- 3 tablespoons Olive oil
- 1 tablespoon Lemon juice
- ½ teaspoon Table salt
- ½ teaspoon Ground black pepper

Directions:
1. Preheat the air fryer to 400°F.
2. Set the pepper(s) in the basket and air-fry undisturbed for 15 minutes, until blistered and even blackened.
3. Use kitchen tongs to transfer the pepper(s) to a zip-closed plastic bag or small bowl. Seal the bag or cover the bowl with plastic wrap. Set aside for 20 minutes.
4. Peel each pepper, then stem it, cut it in half, and remove all its seeds and their white membranes.
5. Set the pieces of the pepper in a food processor. Add the beans, oregano, olive oil, lemon juice, salt, and pepper. Cover and process until smooth, stopping the machine at least once to scrape down the inside of the canister. Scrape the dip into a bowl and serve warm, or cover and refrigerate for up to 3 days (although the dip tastes best if it's allowed to come back to room temperature).

Nutrition Info: Calories per serving: 218; Carbohydrates: 19.6g; Protein: 2.2g; Fat: 11.3g; Sugar: 1.9g; Sodium: 482mg; Fiber: 8g

BREAD AND BREAKFAST

Goat Cheese, Beet, And Kale Frittata

Servings: 6

Cooking Time: 20 Minutes

Ingredients:

- 6 large eggs
- ½ teaspoon garlic powder
- ¼ teaspoon black pepper
- ¼ teaspoon salt
- 1 cup chopped kale
- 1 cup cooked and chopped red beets
- ⅓ cup crumbled goat cheese

Directions:

1. Preheat the air fryer to 320°F.
2. In a medium bowl, whisk the eggs with the garlic powder, pepper, and salt. Mix in the kale, beets, and goat cheese.
3. Spray an oven-safe 7-inch springform pan with cooking spray. Pour the egg mixture into the pan and place it in the air fryer basket.
4. Cook for 20 minutes, or until the internal temperature reaches 145°F.
5. When the frittata is cooked, let it set for 5 minutes before removing from the pan.
6. Slice and serve immediately.

Nutrition Info: Calories per serving: 112; Carbohydrates: 5g; Protein: 8.3g; Fat: 6.8g; Sugar: 3g; Sodium: 284mg; Fiber: 0.8g

Mexican-style Roasted Corn

Servings: 3
Cooking Time: 14 Minutes

Ingredients:
- 3 tablespoons Butter, melted and cooled
- 2 teaspoons Minced garlic
- ¾ teaspoon Ground cumin
- Up to ¾ teaspoon Red pepper flakes
- ¼ teaspoon Table salt
- 3 Cold 4-inch lengths husked and de-silked corn on the cob
- Minced fresh cilantro leaves
- Crumbled queso fresco

Directions:
1. Preheat the air fryer to 400°F.
2. Mix the melted butter, garlic, cumin, red pepper flakes, and salt in a large zip-closed plastic bag. Add the cold corn pieces, seal the bag, and massage the butter mixture into the surface of the corn.
3. When the machine is at temperature, take the pieces of corn out of the plastic bag and put them in the basket with as much air space between the pieces as possible. Air-fry undisturbed for 14 minutes, until golden brown and maybe even charred in a few small spots.
4. Use kitchen tongs to gently transfer the pieces of corn to a serving platter. Sprinkle each piece with the cilantro and queso fresco. Serve warm.

Nutrition Info: Calories per serving: 227; Carbohydrates: 20g; Protein: 4.6g; Fat: 10.8g; Sugar: 4g; Sodium: 294mg; Fiber: 1.9g

Roasted Vegetable Frittata

Servings: 1
Cooking Time: 19 Minutes

Ingredients:

- ½ red or green bell pepper, cut into ½-inch chunks
- 4 button mushrooms, sliced
- ½ cup diced zucchini
- ½ teaspoon chopped fresh oregano or thyme
- 1 teaspoon olive oil
- 3 eggs, beaten
- ½ cup grated Cheddar cheese
- salt and freshly ground black pepper, to taste
- 1 teaspoon butter
- 1 teaspoon chopped fresh parsley

Directions:

1. Preheat the air fryer to 400°F.
2. Toss the peppers, mushrooms, zucchini and oregano with the olive oil and air-fry for 6 minutes, shaking the basket once or twice during the cooking process to redistribute the ingredients.
3. While the vegetables are cooking, beat the eggs well in a bowl, stir in the Cheddar cheese and season with salt and freshly ground black pepper. Add the air-fried vegetables to this bowl when they have finished cooking.
4. Place a 6- or 7-inch non-stick metal cake pan into the air fryer basket with the butter using an aluminum sling to lower the pan into the basket. (Fold a piece of aluminum foil into a strip about 2-inches wide by 24-inches long.) Air-fry for 1 minute at 380°F to melt the butter. Remove the cake pan and rotate the pan to distribute the butter and grease the pan. Pour the egg mixture into the cake pan and return the pan to the air fryer, using the aluminum sling.
5. Air-fry at 380°F for 12 minutes, or until the frittata has puffed up and is lightly browned. Let the frittata sit in the air fryer for 5 minutes to cool to an edible temperature and set up. Remove the cake pan from the air fryer, sprinkle with parsley and serve immediately.

Nutrition Info: Calories per serving: 528; Carbohydrates: 9.2g; Protein: 34.3g; Fat: 40.8g; Sugar: 5g; Sodium: 84mg; Fiber: 2.6g

Sweet Potato-cinnamon Toast

Servings: 6
Cooking Time: 8 Minutes

Ingredients:
- 1 small sweet potato, cut into ⅜-inch slices
- oil for misting
- ground cinnamon

Directions:
1. Preheat air fryer to 390°F.
2. Spray both sides of sweet potato slices with oil. Sprinkle both sides with cinnamon to taste.
3. Place potato slices in air fryer basket in a single layer.
4. Cook for 4 minutes, turn, and cook for 4 more minutes or until potato slices are barely fork tender.

Nutrition Info: Calories per serving: 39; Carbohydrates: 4.5g; Protein: 0.4g; Fat: 2.3g; Sugar: 1.3g; Sodium: 7mg; Fiber: 0.9g

Baked Eggs

Servings: 4
Cooking Time: 6 Minutes

Ingredients:
- 4 large eggs
- ⅛ teaspoon black pepper
- ⅛ teaspoon salt

Directions:
1. Preheat the air fryer to 330°F. Place 4 silicone muffin liners into the air fryer basket.
2. Crack 1 egg at a time into each silicone muffin liner. Sprinkle with black pepper and salt.
3. Bake for 6 minutes. Remove and let cool 2 minutes prior to serving.

Nutrition Info: Calories per serving: 72; Carbohydrates: 0.4g; Protein: 6.3g; Fat: 5g; Sugar: 0.4g; Sodium: 144mg; Fiber: 0g

FISH AND SEAFOOD RECIPES

Salmon Puttanesca En Papillotte With Zucchini

Servings: 2
Cooking Time: 17 Minutes

Ingredients:
- 1 small zucchini, sliced into ¼-inch thick half moons
- 1 teaspoon olive oil
- salt and freshly ground black pepper
- 2 (5-ounce) salmon fillets
- 1 beefsteak tomato, chopped (about 1 cup)
- 1 tablespoon capers, rinsed
- 10 black olives, pitted and sliced
- 2 tablespoons dry vermouth or white wine
- 2 tablespoons butter
- ¼ cup chopped fresh basil, chopped

Directions:
1. Preheat the air fryer to 400°F.
2. Toss the zucchini with the olive oil, salt and freshly ground black pepper. Transfer the zucchini into the air fryer basket and air-fry for 5 minutes, shaking the basket once or twice during the cooking process.
3. Cut out 2 large rectangles of parchment paper – about 13-inches by 15-inches each. Divide the air-fried zucchini between the two pieces of parchment paper, placing the vegetables in the center of each rectangle.
4. Place a fillet of salmon on each pile of zucchini. Season the fish very well with salt and pepper. Toss the tomato, capers, olives and vermouth (or white wine) together in a bowl. Divide the tomato mixture between the two fish packages, placing it on top of the fish fillets and pouring any juice out of the bowl onto the fish. Top each fillet with a tablespoon of butter.
5. Fold up each parchment square. Bring two edges together and fold them over a few times, leaving some space above the fish. Twist the open sides together and upwards so they can serve as handles for the packet, but don't let them extend beyond the top of the air fryer basket.
6. Place the two packages into the air fryer and air-fry at 400°F for 12 minutes. The packages should be puffed up and slightly browned when fully cooked. Once cooked, let the fish sit in the parchment for 2 minutes.
7. Serve the fish in the parchment paper, or if desired, remove the parchment paper before serving. Garnish with a little fresh basil.

Nutrition Info: Calories per serving: 364; Carbohydrates: 5g; Protein: 29g; Fat: 23.1g; Sugar: 2g; Sodium: 384mg; Fiber: 1.9g

Garlic And Dill Salmon

Servings: 2

Cooking Time: 8 Minutes

Ingredients:
- 12 ounces salmon filets with skin
- 2 tablespoons melted butter
- 1 tablespoon extra-virgin olive oil
- 2 garlic cloves, minced
- 1 tablespoon fresh dill
- ½ teaspoon sea salt
- ½ lemon

Directions:
1. Pat the salmon dry with paper towels.
2. In a small bowl, mix together the melted butter, olive oil, garlic, and dill.
3. Sprinkle the top of the salmon with sea salt. Brush all sides of the salmon with the garlic and dill butter.
4. Preheat the air fryer to 350°F.
5. Place the salmon, skin side down, in the air fryer basket. Cook for 6 to 8 minutes, or until the fish flakes in the center.
6. Remove the salmon and plate on a serving platter. Squeeze fresh lemon over the top of the salmon. Serve immediately.

Nutrition Info: Calories per serving: 442; Carbohydrates: 1.9g; Protein: 41.7g; Fat: 30.6g; Sugar: 0g; Sodium: 684mg; Fiber: 0.3g

Shrimp "scampi"

Servings: 4

Cooking Time: 5 Minutes

Ingredients:

- 1½ pounds Large shrimp (20–25 per pound), peeled and deveined
- ¼ cup Olive oil
- 2 tablespoons Minced garlic
- 1 teaspoon Dried oregano
- Up to 1 teaspoon Red pepper flakes
- ½ teaspoon Table salt
- 2 tablespoons White balsamic vinegar (see here)

Directions:

1. Preheat the air fryer to 400°F.
2. Stir the shrimp, olive oil, garlic, oregano, red pepper flakes, and salt in a large bowl until the shrimp are well coated.
3. When the machine is at temperature, transfer the shrimp to the basket. They will overlap and even sit on top of each other. Air-fry for 5 minutes, tossing and rearranging the shrimp twice to make sure the covered surfaces are exposed, until pink and firm.
4. Pour the contents of the basket into a serving bowl. Pour the vinegar over the shrimp while hot and toss to coat.

Nutrition Info: Calories per serving: 321; Carbohydrates: 4.5g; Protein: 39.1g; Fat: 15.1g; Sugar: 0.1g; Sodium: 704mg; Fiber: 0.4g

Lemon-roasted Salmon Fillets

Servings: 3
Cooking Time: 7 Minutes

Ingredients:
- 3 6-ounce skin-on salmon fillets
- Olive oil spray
- 9 Very thin lemon slices
- ¾ teaspoon Ground black pepper
- ¼ teaspoon Table salt

Directions:
1. Preheat the air fryer to 400°F.
2. Generously coat the skin of each of the fillets with olive oil spray. Set the fillets skin side down on your work surface. Place three overlapping lemon slices down the length of each salmon fillet. Sprinkle them with the pepper and salt. Coat lightly with olive oil spray.
3. Use a nonstick-safe spatula to transfer the fillets one by one to the basket, leaving as much air space between them as possible. Air-fry undisturbed for 7 minutes, or until cooked through.
4. Use a nonstick-safe spatula to transfer the fillets to serving plates. Cool for only a minute or two before serving.

Nutrition Info: Calories per serving: 226; Carbohydrates: 0.4g; Protein: 33.1g; Fat: 10.5; Sugar: 0g; Sodium: 269mg; Fiber: 0.1g

Buttery Lobster Tails

Servings: 4
Cooking Time: 6 Minutes

Ingredients:

- 4 6- to 8-ounce shell-on raw lobster tails
- 2 tablespoons Butter, melted and cooled
- 1 teaspoon Lemon juice
- ½ teaspoon Finely grated lemon zest
- ½ teaspoon Garlic powder
- ½ teaspoon Table salt
- ½ teaspoon Ground black pepper

Directions:

1. Preheat the air fryer to 375°F.
2. To give the tails that restaurant look, you need to butterfly the meat. To do so, place a tail on a cutting board so that the shell is convex. Use kitchen shears to cut a line down the middle of the shell from the larger end to the smaller, cutting only the shell and not the meat below, and stopping before the back fins. Pry open the shell, leaving it intact. Use your clean fingers to separate the meat from the shell's sides and bottom, keeping it attached to the shell at the back near the fins. Pull the meat up and out of the shell through the cut line, laying the meat on top of the shell and closing the shell (as well as you can) under the meat. Make two equidistant cuts down the meat from the larger end to near the smaller end, each about ¼ inch deep, for the classic restaurant look on the plate. Repeat this procedure with the remaining tail(s).
3. Stir the butter, lemon juice, zest, garlic powder, salt, and pepper in a small bowl until well combined. Brush this mixture over the lobster meat set atop the shells.
4. When the machine is at temperature, place the tails shell side down in the basket with as much air space between them as possible. Air-fry undisturbed for 6 minutes, or until the lobster meat has pink streaks over it and is firm.
5. Use kitchen tongs to transfer the tails to a wire rack. Cool for only a minute or two before serving.

Nutrition Info: Calories per serving: 179; Carbohydrates: 0.3g; Protein: 27g; Fat: 7g; Sugar: 0g; Sodium: 584mg; Fiber: 0.1g

Butternut Squash–wrapped Halibut Fillets

Servings: 3

Cooking Time: 11 Minutes

Ingredients:
- 15 Long spiralized peeled and seeded butternut squash strands
- 3 5- to 6-ounce skinless halibut fillets
- 3 tablespoons Butter, melted
- ¾ teaspoon Mild paprika
- ¾ teaspoon Table salt
- ¾ teaspoon Ground black pepper

Directions:
1. Preheat the air fryer to 375°F.
2. Hold 5 long butternut squash strands together and wrap them around a fillet. Set it aside and wrap any remaining fillet(s).
3. Mix the melted butter, paprika, salt, and pepper in a small bowl. Brush this mixture over the squash-wrapped fillets on all sides.
4. When the machine is at temperature, set the fillets in the basket with as much air space between them as possible. Air-fry undisturbed for 10 minutes, or until the squash strands have browned but not burned. If the machine is at 360°F, you may need to add 1 minute to the cooking time. In any event, watch the fish carefully after the 8-minute mark.
5. Use a nonstick-safe spatula to gently transfer the fillets to a serving platter or plates. Cool for only a minute or so before serving.

Nutrition Info: Calories per serving: 273; Carbohydrates: 3.4g; Protein: 30.3g; Fat: 15g; Sugar: 0.6g; Sodium: 684mg; Fiber: 0.8g

Black Cod With Grapes, Fennel, Pecans And Kale

Servings: 2
Cooking Time: 15 Minutes

Ingredients:
- 2 (6- to 8-ounce) fillets of black cod (or sablefish)
- salt and freshly ground black pepper
- olive oil
- ½ cup grapes, halved
- 1 small bulb fennel, sliced ¼-inch thick
- ½ cup pecans
- 3 cups shredded kale
- 2 teaspoons white balsamic vinegar or white wine vinegar
- 2 tablespoons extra virgin olive oil

Directions:
1. Preheat the air fryer to 400°F.
2. Season the cod fillets with salt and pepper and drizzle, brush or spray a little olive oil on top. Place the fish, presentation side up (skin side down), into the air fryer basket. Air-fry for 10 minutes.
3. When the fish has finished cooking, remove the fillets to a side plate and loosely tent with foil to rest.
4. Toss the grapes, fennel and pecans in a bowl with a drizzle of olive oil and season with salt and pepper. Add the grapes, fennel and pecans to the air fryer basket and air-fry for 5 minutes at 400°F, shaking the basket once during the cooking time.
5. Transfer the grapes, fennel and pecans to a bowl with the kale. Dress the kale with the balsamic vinegar and olive oil, season to taste with salt and pepper and serve along side the cooked fish.

Nutrition Info: Calories per serving: 531; Carbohydrates: 17.6g; Protein: 36.2g; Fat: 33.1g; Sugar: 4g; Sodium: 184mg; Fiber: 6.1g

Cajun Flounder Fillets

Servings: 2

Cooking Time: 5 Minutes

Ingredients:
- 2 4-ounce skinless flounder fillet(s)
- 2 teaspoons Peanut oil
- 1 teaspoon Purchased or homemade Cajun dried seasoning blend (see the headnote)

Directions:
1. Preheat the air fryer to 400°F.
2. Oil the fillet(s) by drizzling on the peanut oil, then gently rubbing in the oil with your clean, dry fingers. Sprinkle the seasoning blend evenly over both sides of the fillet(s).
3. When the machine is at temperature, set the fillet(s) in the basket. If working with more than one fillet, they should not touch, although they may be quite close together, depending on the basket's size. Air-fry undisturbed for 5 minutes, or until lightly browned and cooked through.
4. Use a nonstick-safe spatula to transfer the fillets to a serving platter or plate(s). Serve at once.

Nutrition Info: Calories per serving: 172; Carbohydrates: 0g; Protein: 27.4g; Fat: 6.2g; Sugar: 0g; Sodium: 144mg; Fiber: 0g

Blackened Red Snapper

Servings: 4
Cooking Time: 8 Minutes

Ingredients:
- 1½ teaspoons black pepper
- ¼ teaspoon thyme
- ¼ teaspoon garlic powder
- ⅛ teaspoon cayenne pepper
- 1 teaspoon olive oil
- 4 4-ounce red snapper fillet portions, skin on
- 4 thin slices lemon
- cooking spray

Directions:
1. Mix the spices and oil together to make a paste. Rub into both sides of the fish.
2. Spray air fryer basket with nonstick cooking spray and lay snapper steaks in basket, skin-side down.
3. Place a lemon slice on each piece of fish.
4. Cook at 390°F for 8 minutes. The fish will not flake when done, but it should be white through the center.

Nutrition Info: Calories per serving: 160; Carbohydrates: 0.7g; Protein: 29.5g; Fat: 3.2g; Sugar: 0.1g; Sodium: 74mg; Fiber: 0.1g

Easy Scallops With Lemon Butter

Servings: 3
Cooking Time: 4 Minutes

Ingredients:
- 1 tablespoon Olive oil
- 2 teaspoons Minced garlic
- 1 teaspoon Finely grated lemon zest
- ½ teaspoon Red pepper flakes
- ¼ teaspoon Table salt
- 1 pound Sea scallops
- 3 tablespoons Butter, melted
- 1½ tablespoons Lemon juice

Directions:
1. Preheat the air fryer to 400°F.
2. Gently stir the olive oil, garlic, lemon zest, red pepper flakes, and salt in a bowl. Add the scallops and stir very gently until they are evenly and well coated.
3. When the machine is at temperature, arrange the scallops in a single layer in the basket. Some may touch. Air-fry undisturbed for 4 minutes, or until the scallops are opaque and firm.
4. While the scallops cook, stir the melted butter and lemon juice in a serving bowl. When the scallops are ready, pour them from the basket into this bowl. Toss well before serving.

Nutrition Info: Calories per serving: 281; Carbohydrates: 4.7g; Protein: 25.7g; Fat: 17.1g; Sugar: 0.3g; Sodium: 514mg; Fiber: 0.2g

Italian Tuna Roast

Servings: 8
Cooking Time: 21 Minutes

Ingredients:
- cooking spray
- 1 tablespoon Italian seasoning
- ⅛ teaspoon ground black pepper
- 1 tablespoon extra-light olive oil
- 1 teaspoon lemon juice
- 1 tuna loin (approximately 2 pounds, 3 to 4 inches thick, large enough to fill a 6 x 6-inch baking dish)

Directions:
1. Spray baking dish with cooking spray and place in air fryer basket. Preheat air fryer to 390°F.
2. Mix together the Italian seasoning, pepper, oil, and lemon juice.
3. Using a dull table knife or butter knife, pierce top of tuna about every half inch: Insert knife into top of tuna roast and pierce almost all the way to the bottom.
4. Spoon oil mixture into each of the holes and use the knife to push seasonings into the tuna as deeply as possible.
5. Spread any remaining oil mixture on all outer surfaces of tuna.
6. Place tuna roast in baking dish and cook at 390°F for 20 minutes. Check temperature with a meat thermometer. Cook for an additional 1 minutes or until temperature reaches 145°F.
7. Remove basket from fryer and let tuna sit in basket for 10minutes.

Nutrition Info: Calories per serving: 231; Carbohydrates: 0.2g; Protein: 30.1g; Fat: 11.4g; Sugar: 0.2g; Sodium: 64mg; Fiber: 0g

Pecan-crusted Tilapia

Servings: 4
Cooking Time: 8 Minutes

Ingredients:
- 1 pound skinless, boneless tilapia filets
- ¼ cup butter, melted
- 1 teaspoon minced fresh or dried rosemary
- 1 cup finely chopped pecans
- 1 teaspoon sea salt
- ¼ teaspoon paprika
- 2 tablespoons chopped parsley
- 1 lemon, cut into wedges

Directions:
1. Pat the tilapia filets dry with paper towels.
2. Pour the melted butter over the filets and flip the filets to coat them completely.
3. In a medium bowl, mix together the rosemary, pecans, salt, and paprika.
4. Preheat the air fryer to 350°F.
5. Place the tilapia filets into the air fryer basket and top with the pecan coating. Cook for 6 to 8 minutes. The fish should be firm to the touch and flake easily when fully cooked.
6. Remove the fish from the air fryer. Top the fish with chopped parsley and serve with lemon wedges.

Nutrition Info: Calories per serving: 415; Carbohydrates: 4.9g; Protein: 24.7g; Fat: 33.1g; Sugar: 1.2g; Sodium: 584mg; Fiber: 3.6g

Sesame-crusted Tuna Steaks

Servings: 3
Cooking Time: 10-13 Minutes

Ingredients:
- ½ cup Sesame seeds, preferably a blend of white and black
- 1½ tablespoons Toasted sesame oil
- 3 6-ounce skinless tuna steaks

Directions:
1. Preheat the air fryer to 400°F.
2. Pour the sesame seeds on a dinner plate. Use ½ tablespoon of the sesame oil as a rub on both sides and the edges of a tuna steak. Set it in the sesame seeds, then turn it several times, pressing gently, to create an even coating of the seeds, including around the steak's edge. Set aside and continue coating the remaining steak(s).
3. When the machine is at temperature, set the steaks in the basket with as much air space between them as possible. Air-fry undisturbed for 10 minutes for medium-rare (not USDA-approved), or 12 to 13 minutes for cooked through (USDA-approved).
4. Use a nonstick-safe spatula to transfer the steaks to serving plates. Serve hot.

Nutrition Info: Calories per serving: 356; Carbohydrates: 4.6g; Protein: 43.1g; Fat: 17.3g; Sugar: 0.1g; Sodium: 184mg; Fiber: 0.1g

Sweet Potato-wrapped Shrimp

Servings: 3

Cooking Time: 6 Minutes

Ingredients:
- 24 Long spiralized sweet potato strands
- Olive oil spray
- ¼ teaspoon Garlic powder
- ¼ teaspoon Table salt
- Up to a ⅛ teaspoon Cayenne
- 12 Large shrimp (20–25 per pound), peeled and deveined

Directions:
1. Preheat the air fryer to 400°F.
2. Lay the spiralized sweet potato strands on a large swath of paper towels and straighten out the strands to long ropes. Coat them with olive oil spray, then sprinkle them with the garlic powder, salt, and cayenne.
3. Pick up 2 strands and wrap them around the center of a shrimp, with the ends tucked under what now becomes the bottom side of the shrimp. Continue wrapping the remainder of the shrimp.
4. Set the shrimp bottom side down in the basket with as much air space between them as possible. Air-fry undisturbed for 6 minutes, or until the sweet potato strands are crisp and the shrimp are pink and firm.
5. Use kitchen tongs to transfer the shrimp to a wire rack. Cool for only a minute or two before serving.

Nutrition Info: Calories per serving: 135; Carbohydrates: 8.4g; Protein: 20.8g; Fat: 1.6g; Sugar: 2.2g; Sodium: 421mg; Fiber: 1.1g

Blackened Catfish

Servings: 4
Cooking Time: 8 Minutes

Ingredients:

- 1 teaspoon paprika
- 1 teaspoon garlic powder
- 1 teaspoon onion powder
- 1 teaspoon ground dried thyme
- ½ teaspoon ground black pepper
- ⅛ teaspoon cayenne pepper
- ½ teaspoon dried oregano
- ⅛ teaspoon crushed red pepper flakes
- 1 pound catfish filets
- ½ teaspoon sea salt
- 2 tablespoons butter, melted
- 1 tablespoon extra-virgin olive oil
- 2 tablespoons chopped parsley
- 1 lemon, cut into wedges

Directions:

1. In a small bowl, stir together the paprika, garlic powder, onion powder, thyme, black pepper, cayenne pepper, oregano, and crushed red pepper flakes.
2. Pat the fish dry with paper towels. Season the filets with sea salt and then coat with the blackening seasoning.
3. In a small bowl, mix together the butter and olive oil and drizzle over the fish filets, flipping them to coat them fully.
4. Preheat the air fryer to 350°F.
5. Place the fish in the air fryer basket and cook for 8 minutes, checking the fish for doneness after 4 minutes. The fish will flake easily when cooked.
6. Remove the fish from the air fryer. Top with chopped parsley and serve with lemon wedges.

Nutrition Info: Calories per serving: 242; Carbohydrates: 1.7g; Protein: 18.1g; Fat: 18g; Sugar: 0.5g; Sodium: 337mg; Fiber: 0.5g

Lobster Tails With Lemon Garlic Butter

Servings: 2

Cooking Time: 5 Minutes

Ingredients:

- 4 ounces unsalted butter
- 1 tablespoon finely chopped lemon zest
- 1 clove garlic, thinly sliced
- 2 (6-ounce) lobster tails
- salt and freshly ground black pepper
- ½ cup white wine
- ½ lemon, sliced
- vegetable oil

Directions:

1. Start by making the lemon garlic butter. Combine the butter, lemon zest and garlic in a small saucepan. Melt and simmer the butter on the stovetop over the lowest possible heat while you prepare the lobster tails.

2. Prepare the lobster tails by cutting down the middle of the top of the shell. Crack the bottom shell by squeezing the sides of the lobster together so that you can access the lobster meat inside. Pull the lobster tail up out of the shell, but leave it attached at the base of the tail. Lay the lobster meat on top of the shell and season with salt and freshly ground black pepper. Pour a little of the lemon garlic butter on top of the lobster meat and transfer the lobster to the refrigerator so that the butter solidifies a little.

3. Pour the white wine into the air fryer drawer and add the lemon slices. Preheat the air fryer to 400°F for 5 minutes.

4. Transfer the lobster tails to the air fryer basket. Air-fry at 370° for 5 minutes, brushing more butter on halfway through cooking. (Add a minute or two if your lobster tail is more than 6-ounces.) Remove and serve with more butter for dipping or drizzling.

Nutrition Info: Calories per serving: 612; Carbohydrates: 2.8g; Protein: 33g; Fat: 45g; Sugar: 0.7g; Sodium: 784mg; Fiber: 0.2g

Five Spice Red Snapper With Green Onions And Orange Salsa

Servings: 2
Cooking Time: 8 Minutes

Ingredients:
- 2 oranges, peeled, segmented and chopped
- 1 tablespoon minced shallot
- 1 to 3 teaspoons minced red Jalapeño or Serrano pepper
- 1 tablespoon chopped fresh cilantro
- lime juice, to taste
- salt, to taste
- 2 (5- to 6-ounce) red snapper fillets
- ½ teaspoon Chinese five spice powder
- salt and freshly ground black pepper
- vegetable or olive oil, in a spray bottle
- 4 green onions, cut into 2-inch lengths

Directions:
1. Start by making the salsa. Cut the peel off the oranges, slicing around the oranges to expose the flesh. Segment the oranges by cutting in between the membranes of the orange. Chop the segments roughly and combine in a bowl with the shallot, Jalapeño or Serrano pepper, cilantro, lime juice and salt. Set the salsa aside.
2. Preheat the air fryer to 400°F.
3. Season the fish fillets with the five-spice powder, salt and freshly ground black pepper. Spray both sides of the fish fillets with oil. Toss the green onions with a little oil.
4. Transfer the fish to the air fryer basket and scatter the green onions around the fish. Air-fry at 400°F for 8 minutes.
5. Remove the fish from the air fryer, along with the fried green onions. Serve with white rice and a spoonful of the salsa on top.

Nutrition Info: Calories per serving: 318; Carbohydrates: 19.6g; Protein: 2.2g; Fat: 3.2g; Sugar: 7g; Sodium: 184mg; Fiber: 4.2g

Quick Shrimp Scampi

Servings: 2
Cooking Time: 5 Minutes

Ingredients:
- 16 to 20 raw large shrimp, peeled, deveined and tails removed
- ½ cup white wine
- freshly ground black pepper
- ¼ cup + 1 tablespoon butter, divided
- 1 clove garlic, sliced
- 1 teaspoon olive oil
- salt, to taste
- juice of ½ lemon, to taste
- ¼ cup chopped fresh parsley

Directions:

1. Start by marinating the shrimp in the white wine and freshly ground black pepper for at least 30 minutes, or as long as 2 hours in the refrigerator.
2. Preheat the air fryer to 400°F.
3. Melt ¼ cup of butter in a small saucepan on the stovetop. Add the garlic and let the butter simmer, but be sure to not let it burn.
4. Pour the shrimp and marinade into the air fryer, letting the marinade drain through to the bottom drawer. Drizzle the olive oil on the shrimp and season well with salt. Air-fry at 400°F for 3 minutes. Turn the shrimp over (don't shake the basket because the marinade will splash around) and pour the garlic butter over the shrimp. Air-fry for another 2 minutes.
5. Remove the shrimp from the air fryer basket and transfer them to a bowl. Squeeze lemon juice over all the shrimp and toss with the chopped parsley and remaining tablespoon of butter. Season to taste with salt and serve immediately.

Nutrition Info: Calories per serving: 488; Carbohydrates: 5g; Protein: 40.8g; Fat: 23.1g; Sugar: 0.7g; Sodium: 674mg; Fiber: 0.3g

Crab Stuffed Salmon Roast

Servings: 4
Cooking Time: 20 Minutes

Ingredients:

- 1 (1½-pound) salmon fillet
- salt and freshly ground black pepper
- 6 ounces crabmeat
- 1 teaspoon finely chopped lemon zest
- 1 teaspoon Dijon mustard
- 1 tablespoon chopped fresh parsley, plus more for garnish
- 1 scallion, chopped
- ¼ teaspoon salt
- olive oil

Directions:

1. Prepare the salmon fillet by butterflying it. Slice into the thickest side of the salmon, parallel to the countertop and along the length of the fillet. Don't slice all the way through to the other side – stop about an inch from the edge. Open the salmon up like a book. Season the salmon with salt and freshly ground black pepper.
2. Make the crab filling by combining the crabmeat, lemon zest, mustard, parsley, scallion, salt and freshly ground black pepper in a bowl. Spread this filling in the center of the salmon. Fold one side of the salmon over the filling. Then fold the other side over on top.
3. Transfer the rolled salmon to the center of a piece of parchment paper that is roughly 6- to 7-inches wide and about 12-inches long. The parchment paper will act as a sling, making it easier to put the salmon into the air fryer. Preheat the air fryer to 370°F. Use the parchment paper to transfer the salmon roast to the air fryer basket and tuck the ends of the paper down beside the salmon. Drizzle a little olive oil on top and season with salt and pepper.
4. Air-fry the salmon at 370°F for 20 minutes.
5. Remove the roast from the air fryer and let it rest for a few minutes. Then, slice it, sprinkle some more lemon zest and parsley (or fresh chives) on top and serve.

Nutrition Info: Calories per serving: 266; Carbohydrates: 1.3g; Protein: 38.5g; Fat: 11.3g; Sugar: 0.1g; Sodium: 504mg; Fiber: 0.2g

VEGETARIANS RECIPES

Vegetable Couscous

Servings: 4
Cooking Time: 10 Minutes

Ingredients:
- 4 ounces white mushrooms, sliced
- ½ medium green bell pepper, julienned
- 1 cup cubed zucchini
- ¼ small onion, slivered
- 1 stalk celery, thinly sliced
- ¼ teaspoon ground coriander
- ¼ teaspoon ground cumin
- salt and pepper
- 1 tablespoon olive oil
- Couscous
- ¾ cup uncooked couscous
- 1 cup vegetable broth or water
- ½ teaspoon salt (omit if using salted broth)

Directions:
1. Combine all vegetables in large bowl. Sprinkle with coriander, cumin, and salt and pepper to taste. Stir well, add olive oil, and stir again to coat vegetables evenly.
2. Place vegetables in air fryer basket and cook at 390°F for 5minutes. Stir and cook for 5 more minutes, until tender.
3. While vegetables are cooking, prepare the couscous: Place broth or water and salt in large saucepan. Heat to boiling, stir in couscous, cover, and remove from heat.
4. Let couscous sit for 5minutes, stir in cooked vegetables, and serve hot.

Nutrition Info: Calories per serving: 168; Carbohydrates: 19.6g; Protein: 5.6g; Fat: 3.9g; Sugar: 1.6g; Sodium: 84mg; Fiber: 2g

Lentil Fritters

Servings: 9
Cooking Time: 12 Minutes

Ingredients:
- 1 cup cooked red lentils
- 1 cup riced cauliflower
- ½ medium zucchini, shredded (about 1 cup)
- ¼ cup finely chopped onion
- ¼ teaspoon salt
- ¼ teaspoon black pepper
- ½ teaspoon garlic powder
- ¼ teaspoon paprika
- 1 large egg
- ⅓ cup quinoa flour

Directions:
1. Preheat the air fryer to 370°F.
2. In a large bowl, mix the lentils, cauliflower, zucchini, onion, salt, pepper, garlic powder, and paprika. Mix in the egg and flour until a thick dough forms.
3. Using a large spoon, form the dough into 9 large fritters.
4. Liberally spray the air fryer basket with olive oil. Place the fritters into the basket, leaving space around each fritter so you can flip them.
5. Cook for 6 minutes, flip, and cook another 6 minutes.
6. Remove from the air fryer and repeat with the remaining fritters. Serve warm with desired sauce and sides.

Nutrition Info: Calories per serving: 49; Carbohydrates: 9g; Protein: 3g; Fat: 0.4g; Sugar: 1.1g; Sodium: 84mg; Fiber: 2.3g

Pizza Portobello Mushrooms

Servings: 2
Cooking Time: 18 Minutes

Ingredients:

- 2 portobello mushroom caps, gills removed (see Figure 13-1)
- 1 teaspoon extra-virgin olive oil
- ¼ cup diced onion
- 1 teaspoon minced garlic
- 1 medium zucchini, shredded
- 1 teaspoon dried oregano
- ½ teaspoon black pepper
- ¼ teaspoon salt
- ⅓ cup sugar-free marinara sauce
- ¼ cup shredded part-skim mozzarella cheese
- ¼ teaspoon red pepper flakes
- 2 tablespoons Parmesan cheese
- 2 tablespoons chopped basil

Directions:

1. Preheat the air fryer to 370°F.
2. Lightly spray the mushrooms with an olive oil mist and place into the air fryer to cook for 10 minutes, cap side up.
3. Add the olive oil to a pan and sauté the onion and garlic together for about 2 to 4 minutes. Stir in the zucchini, oregano, pepper, and salt, and continue to cook. When the zucchini has cooked down (usually about 4 to 6 minutes), add in the marinara sauce. Remove from the heat and stir in the mozzarella cheese.
4. Remove the mushrooms from the air fryer basket when cooking completes. Reset the temperature to 350°F.
5. Using a spoon, carefully stuff the mushrooms with the zucchini marinara mixture.
6. Return the stuffed mushrooms to the air fryer basket and cook for 5 to 8 minutes, or until the cheese is lightly browned. You should be able to easily insert a fork into the mushrooms when they're cooked.
7. Remove the mushrooms and sprinkle the red pepper flakes, Parmesan cheese, and fresh basil over the top.
8. Serve warm.

Nutrition Info: Calories per serving: 120; Carbohydrates: 11.6g; Protein: 8.7g; Fat: 5.7g; Sugar: 4g; Sodium: 484mg; Fiber: 3g

Veggie Fried Rice

Servings: 4
Cooking Time: 25 Minutes

Ingredients:

- 1 cup cooked brown rice
- ⅓ cup chopped onion
- ½ cup chopped carrots
- ½ cup chopped bell peppers
- ½ cup chopped broccoli florets
- 3 tablespoons low-sodium soy sauce
- 1 tablespoon sesame oil
- 1 teaspoon ground ginger
- 1 teaspoon ground garlic powder
- ½ teaspoon black pepper
- ⅛ teaspoon salt
- 2 large eggs

Directions:

1. Preheat the air fryer to 370°F.
2. In a large bowl, mix together the brown rice, onions, carrots, bell pepper, and broccoli.
3. In a small bowl, whisk together the soy sauce, sesame oil, ginger, garlic powder, pepper, salt, and eggs.
4. Pour the egg mixture into the rice and vegetable mixture and mix together.
5. Liberally spray a 7-inch springform pan (or compatible air fryer dish) with olive oil. Add the rice mixture to the pan and cover with aluminum foil.
6. Place a metal trivet into the air fryer basket and set the pan on top. Cook for 15 minutes. Carefully remove the pan from basket, discard the foil, and mix the rice. Return the rice to the air fryer basket, turning down the temperature to 350°F and cooking another 10 minutes.
7. Remove and let cool 5 minutes. Serve warm.

Nutrition Info: Calories per serving: 140; Carbohydrates: 16g; Protein: 5.7g; Fat: 6.3g; Sugar: 2.7g; Sodium: 704mg; Fiber: 1.6g

BEEF, PORK & LAMB RECIPES

Beef And Spinach Braciole

Servings: 4
Cooking Time: 92 Minutes

Ingredients:

- 7-inch oven-safe baking pan or casserole
- ½ onion, finely chopped
- 1 teaspoon olive oil
- ⅓ cup red wine
- 2 cups crushed tomatoes
- 1 teaspoon Italian seasoning
- ½ teaspoon garlic powder
- ¼ teaspoon crushed red pepper flakes
- 2 tablespoons chopped fresh parsley
- 2 top round steaks (about 1½ pounds)
- salt and freshly ground black pepper
- 2 cups fresh spinach, chopped
- 1 clove minced garlic
- ½ cup roasted red peppers, julienned
- ½ cup grated pecorino cheese
- ¼ cup pine nuts, toasted and rough chopped
- 2 tablespoons olive oil

Directions:

1. Preheat the air fryer to 400°F.
2. Toss the onions and olive oil together in a 7-inch metal baking pan or casserole dish. Air-fry at 400°F for 5 minutes, stirring a couple times during the cooking process. Add the red wine, crushed tomatoes, Italian seasoning, garlic powder, red pepper flakes and parsley and stir. Cover the pan tightly with aluminum foil, lower the air fryer temperature to 350°F and continue to air-fry for 15 minutes.
3. While the sauce is simmering, prepare the beef. Using a meat mallet, pound the beef until it is ¼-inch thick. Season both sides of the beef with salt and pepper. Combine the spinach, garlic, red peppers, pecorino cheese, pine nuts and olive oil in a medium bowl. Season with salt and freshly ground black pepper. Spread the mixture evenly over the steaks. Starting at one of the short ends, roll the beef around the filling, tucking in the sides as you roll to ensure the filling is completely enclosed. Secure the beef rolls with toothpicks.
4. Remove the baking pan with the sauce from the air fryer and set it aside. Preheat the air fryer to 400°F.
5. Brush or spray the beef rolls with a little olive oil and air-fry at 400°F for 12 minutes, rotating the beef during the cooking process for even browning. When the beef is browned, submerge the

rolls into the sauce in the baking pan, cover the pan with foil and return it to the air fryer. Air-fry at 250°F for 60 minutes.

6. Remove the beef rolls from the sauce. Cut each roll into slices and serve with pasta, ladling some of the sauce overtop.

Nutrition Info: Calories per serving: 462; Carbohydrates: 9.1g; Protein: 46.1g; Fat: 25g; Sugar: 4.7g; Sodium: 452mg; Fiber: 2.4g

Almond And Sun-dried Tomato Crusted Pork Chops

Servings: 4
Cooking Time: 10 Minutes

Ingredients:

- ½ cup oil-packed sun-dried tomatoes
- ½ cup toasted almonds
- ¼ cup grated Parmesan cheese
- ½ cup olive oil
- 2 tablespoons water
- ½ teaspoon salt
- freshly ground black pepper
- 4 center-cut boneless pork chops (about 1¼ pounds)

Directions:

1. Place the sun-dried tomatoes into a food processor and pulse them until they are coarsely chopped. Add the almonds, Parmesan cheese, olive oil, water, salt and pepper. Process all the ingredients into a smooth paste. Spread most of the paste (leave a little in reserve) onto both sides of the pork chops and then pierce the meat several times with a needle-style meat tenderizer or a fork. Let the pork chops sit and marinate for at least 1 hour (refrigerate if marinating for longer than 1 hour).
2. Preheat the air fryer to 370°F.
3. Brush a little olive oil on the bottom of the air fryer basket. Transfer the pork chops into the air fryer basket, spooning a little more of the sun-dried tomato paste onto the pork chops if there are any gaps where the paste may have been rubbed off. Air-fry the pork chops at 370°F for 10 minutes, turning the chops over halfway through the cooking process.
4. When the pork chops have finished cooking, transfer them to a serving plate and serve with mashed potatoes and vegetables for a hearty meal.

Nutrition Info: Calories per serving: 535; Carbohydrates: 5.8g; Protein: 42.3g; Fat: 39.3g; Sugar: 0.5g; Sodium: 451mg; Fiber: 2.3g

Pork Chops

Servings: 2
Cooking Time: 16 Minutes

Ingredients:

- 2 bone-in, centercut pork chops, 1-inch thick (10 ounces each)
- 2 teaspoons Worcestershire sauce
- salt and pepper
- cooking spray

Directions:

1. Rub the Worcestershire sauce into both sides of pork chops.
2. Season with salt and pepper to taste.
3. Spray air fryer basket with cooking spray and place the chops in basket side by side.
4. Cook at 360°F for 16 minutes or until well done. Let rest for 5minutes before serving.

Nutrition Info: Calories per serving: 609; Carbohydrates: 1g; Protein: 80.7g; Fat: 28.7g; Sugar: 1g; Sodium: 259mg; Fiber: 0g

Rosemary Lamb Chops

Servings: 4
Cooking Time: 6 Minutes

Ingredients:

- 8 lamb chops
- 1 tablespoon extra-virgin olive oil
- 1 teaspoon dried rosemary, crushed
- 2 cloves garlic, minced
- 1 teaspoon sea salt
- ¼ teaspoon black pepper

Directions:

1. In a large bowl, mix together the lamb chops, olive oil, rosemary, garlic, salt, and pepper. Let sit at room temperature for 10 minutes.
2. Meanwhile, preheat the air fryer to 380°F.
3. Cook the lamb chops for 3 minutes, flip them over, and cook for another 3 minutes.

Nutrition Info: Calories per serving: 455; Carbohydrates: 0.8g; Protein: 63.8g; Fat: 20.2g; Sugar: 0g; Sodium: 754mg; Fiber: 0.2g

Carne Asada

Servings: 4
Cooking Time: 15 Minutes

Ingredients:

- 4 cloves garlic, minced
- 3 chipotle peppers in adobo, chopped
- ⅓ cup chopped fresh parsley
- ⅓ cup chopped fresh oregano
- 1 teaspoon ground cumin seed
- juice of 2 limes
- ⅓ cup olive oil
- 1 to 1½ pounds flank steak (depending on your appetites)
- salt
- guacamole (optional – for serving)

Directions:

1. Make the marinade: Combine the garlic, chipotle, parsley, oregano, cumin, lime juice and olive oil in a non-reactive bowl. Coat the flank steak with the marinade and let it marinate for 30 minutes to 8 hours. (Don't leave the steak out of refrigeration for longer than 2 hours, however.)
2. Preheat the air fryer to 390°F.
3. Remove the steak from the marinade and place it in the air fryer basket. Season the steak with salt and air-fry for 15 minutes, turning the steak over halfway through the cooking time and seasoning again with salt. This should cook the steak to medium. Add or subtract two minutes for medium-well or medium-rare.
4. Remember to let the steak rest before slicing the meat against the grain. Serve with warm tortillas, guacamole and a fresh salsa like the Tomato-Corn Salsa below.

Nutrition Info: Calories per serving: 505; Carbohydrates: 5.6g; Protein: 48.3g; Fat: 31.6g; Sugar: 0.8g; Sodium: 208mg; Fiber: 3.8g

Barbecue-style London Broil

Servings: 5
Cooking Time: 17 Minutes

Ingredients:

- ¾ teaspoon Mild smoked paprika
- ¾ teaspoon Dried oregano
- ¾ teaspoon Table salt
- ¾ teaspoon Ground black pepper
- ¼ teaspoon Garlic powder
- ¼ teaspoon Onion powder
- 1½ pounds Beef London broil (in one piece)
- Olive oil spray

Directions:

1. Preheat the air fryer to 400°F.

2. Mix the smoked paprika, oregano, salt, pepper, garlic powder, and onion powder in a small bowl until uniform.

3. Pat and rub this mixture across all surfaces of the beef. Lightly coat the beef on all sides with olive oil spray.

4. When the machine is at temperature, lay the London broil flat in the basket and air-fry undisturbed for 8 minutes for the small batch, 10 minutes for the medium batch, or 12 minutes for the large batch for medium-rare, until an instant-read meat thermometer inserted into the center of the meat registers 130°F (not USDA-approved). Add 1, 2, or 3 minutes, respectively (based on the size of the cut) for medium, until an instant-read meat thermometer registers 135°F (not USDA-approved). Or add 3, 4, or 5 minutes respectively for medium, until an instant-read meat thermometer registers 145°F (USDA-approved).

5. Use kitchen tongs to transfer the London broil to a cutting board. Let the meat rest for 10 minutes. It needs a long time for the juices to be reincorporated into the meat's fibers. Carve it against the grain into very thin (less than ¼-inch-thick) slices to serve.

Nutrition Info: Calories per serving: 184; Carbohydrates: 0.7g; Protein: 30.3g; Fat: 6.1g; Sugar: 0.1g; Sodium: 427mg; Fiber: 0.3g

Lemon-butter Veal Cutlets

Servings: 2
Cooking Time: 4 Minutes

Ingredients:
- 3 strips Butter (see step 2)
- 3 Thinly pounded 2-ounce veal leg cutlets (less than ¼ inch thick)
- ¼ teaspoon Lemon-pepper seasoning

Directions:
1. Preheat the air fryer to 400°F.
2. Run a vegetable peeler lengthwise along a hard, cold stick of butter, making 2, 3, or 4 long strips as the recipe requires for the number of cutlets you're making.
3. Lay the veal cutlets on a clean, dry cutting board or work surface. Sprinkle about ⅛ teaspoon lemon-pepper seasoning over each. Set a strip of butter on top of each cutlet.
4. When the machine is at temperature, set the topped cutlets in the basket so that they don't overlap or even touch. Air-fry undisturbed for 4 minutes without turning.
5. Use a nonstick-safe spatula to transfer the cutlets to a serving plate or plates, taking care to keep as much of the butter on top as possible. Remove the basket from the drawer or from over the baking tray. Carefully pour the browned butter over the cutlets.

Nutrition Info: Calories per serving: 248; Carbohydrates: 0.2g; Protein: 25.7g; Fat: 15.1g; Sugar: 0g; Sodium: 115mg; Fiber: 0.1g

Perfect Pork Chops

Servings: 3
Cooking Time: 10 Minutes

Ingredients:
- ¾ teaspoon Mild paprika
- ¾ teaspoon Dried thyme
- ¾ teaspoon Onion powder
- ¼ teaspoon Garlic powder
- ¼ teaspoon Table salt
- ¼ teaspoon Ground black pepper
- 3 6-ounce boneless center-cut pork loin chops
- Vegetable oil spray

Directions:
1. Preheat the air fryer to 400°F.
2. Mix the paprika, thyme, onion powder, garlic powder, salt, and pepper in a small bowl until well combined. Massage this mixture into both sides of the chops. Generously coat both sides of the chops with vegetable oil spray.
3. When the machine is at temperature, set the chops in the basket with as much air space between them as possible. Air-fry undisturbed for 10 minutes, or until an instant-read meat thermometer inserted into the thickest part of a chop registers 145°F.
4. Use kitchen tongs to transfer the chops to a cutting board or serving plates. Cool for 5 minutes before serving.

Nutrition Info: Calories per serving: 249; Carbohydrates: 1.2g; Protein: 44.7g; Fat: 6.1g; Sugar: 0.3g; Sodium: 292mg; Fiber: 0.4g

Balsamic Marinated Rib Eye Steak With Balsamic Fried Cipollini Onions

Servings: 3
Cooking Time: 22-26 Minutes

Ingredients:

- 3 tablespoons balsamic vinegar
- 2 cloves garlic, sliced
- 1 tablespoon Dijon mustard
- 1 teaspoon fresh thyme leaves
- 1 (16-ounce) boneless rib eye steak
- coarsely ground black pepper
- salt
- 1 (8-ounce) bag cipollini onions, peeled
- 1 teaspoon balsamic vinegar

Directions:

1. Combine the 3 tablespoons of balsamic vinegar, garlic, Dijon mustard and thyme in a small bowl. Pour this marinade over the steak. Pierce the steak several times with a paring knife or
2. a needle-style meat tenderizer and season it generously with coarsely ground black pepper. Flip the steak over and pierce the other side in a similar fashion, seasoning again with the coarsely ground black pepper. Marinate the steak for 2 to 24 hours in the refrigerator. When you are ready to cook, remove the steak from the refrigerator and let it sit at room temperature for 30 minutes.
3. Preheat the air fryer to 400°F.
4. Season the steak with salt and air-fry at 400°F for 12 minutes (medium-rare), 14 minutes (medium), or 16 minutes (well-done), flipping the steak once half way through the cooking time.
5. While the steak is air-frying, toss the onions with 1 teaspoon of balsamic vinegar and season with salt.
6. Remove the steak from the air fryer and let it rest while you fry the onions. Transfer the onions to the air fryer basket and air-fry for 10 minutes, adding a few more minutes if your onions are very large. Then, slice the steak on the bias and serve with the fried onions on top.

Nutrition Info: Calories per serving: 454; Carbohydrates: 8g; Protein: 42.4g; Fat: 27.3g; Sugar: 3g; Sodium: 148mg; Fiber: 1.3g

Beef Al Carbon (street Taco Meat)

Servings: 6
Cooking Time: 8 Minutes

Ingredients:

- 1½ pounds sirloin steak, cut into ½-inch cubes
- ¾ cup lime juice
- ½ cup extra-virgin olive oil
- 1 teaspoon ground cumin
- 2 teaspoons garlic powder
- 1 teaspoon salt

Directions:

1. In a large bowl, toss together the steak, lime juice, olive oil, cumin, garlic powder, and salt. Allow the meat to marinate for 30 minutes. Drain off all the marinade and pat the meat dry with paper towels.
2. Preheat the air fryer to 400°F.
3. Place the meat in the air fryer basket and spray with cooking spray. Cook the meat for 5 minutes, toss the meat, and continue cooking another 3 minutes, until slightly crispy.

Nutrition Info: Calories per serving: 362; Carbohydrates: 1.1g; Protein: 34.6g; Fat: 24g; Sugar: 0.2g; Sodium: 463mg; Fiber: 0.1g

Mustard-crusted Rib-eye

Servings: 2
Cooking Time: 9 Minutes

Ingredients:

- Two 6-ounce rib-eye steaks, about 1-inch thick
- 1 teaspoon coarse salt
- ½ teaspoon coarse black pepper
- 2 tablespoons Dijon mustard

Directions:

1. Rub the steaks with the salt and pepper. Then spread the mustard on both sides of the steaks. Cover with foil and let the steaks sit at room temperature for 30 minutes.
2. Preheat the air fryer to 390°F.
3. Cook the steaks for 9 minutes. Check for an internal temperature of 140°F and immediately remove the steaks and let them rest for 5 minutes before slicing.

Nutrition Info: Calories per serving: 478; Carbohydrates: 1.2g; Protein: 30.9g; Fat: 38.3g; Sugar: 0.1g; Sodium: 784mg; Fiber: 0.7g

Pesto-rubbed Veal Chops

Servings: 2
Cooking Time: 12-15 Minutes

Ingredients:
- ¼ cup Purchased pesto
- 2 10-ounce bone-in veal loin or rib chop(s)
- ½ teaspoon Ground black pepper

Directions:
1. Preheat the air fryer to 400°F.
2. Rub the pesto onto both sides of the veal chop(s). Sprinkle one side of the chop(s) with the ground black pepper. Set aside at room temperature as the machine comes up to temperature.
3. Set the chop(s) in the basket. If you're cooking more than one chop, leave as much air space between them as possible. Air-fry undisturbed for 12 minutes for medium-rare, or until an instant-read meat thermometer inserted into the center of a chop (without touching bone) registers 135°F (not USDA-approved). Or air-fry undisturbed for 15 minutes for medium-well, or until an instant-read meat thermometer registers 145°F (USDA-approved).
4. Use kitchen tongs to transfer the chops to a cutting board or a wire rack. Cool for 5 minutes before serving.

Nutrition Info: Calories per serving: 588; Carbohydrates: 2.3g; Protein: 55.8g; Fat: 38.1g; Sugar: 2g; Sodium: 429mg; Fiber: 0.6g

Boneless Ribeyes

Servings: 2
Cooking Time: 10-15 Minutes

Ingredients:
- 2 8-ounce boneless ribeye steaks
- 4 teaspoons Worcestershire sauce
- ½ teaspoon garlic powder
- pepper
- 4 teaspoons extra virgin olive oil
- salt

Directions:
1. Season steaks on both sides with Worcestershire sauce. Use the back of a spoon to spread evenly.
2. Sprinkle both sides of steaks with garlic powder and coarsely ground black pepper to taste.
3. Drizzle both sides of steaks with olive oil, again using the back of a spoon to spread evenly over surfaces.
4. Allow steaks to marinate for 30minutes.
5. Place both steaks in air fryer basket and cook at 390°F for 5minutes.
6. Turn steaks over and cook until done:
7. Medium rare: additional 5 minutes
8. Medium: additional 7 minutes
9. Well done: additional 10 minutes
10. Remove steaks from air fryer basket and let sit 5minutes. Salt to taste and serve.

Nutrition Info: Calories per serving: 708; Carbohydrates: 2.5g; Protein: 61.7g; Fat: 49.9g; Sugar: 2.2g; Sodium: 242mg; Fiber: 0.1g

Lamb Chops

Servings: 2
Cooking Time: 20 Minutes

Ingredients:
- 2 teaspoons oil
- ½ teaspoon ground rosemary
- ½ teaspoon lemon juice
- 1 pound lamb chops, approximately 1-inch thick
- salt and pepper
- cooking spray

Directions:
1. Mix the oil, rosemary, and lemon juice together and rub into all sides of the lamb chops. Season to taste with salt and pepper.
2. For best flavor, cover lamb chops and allow them to rest in the fridge for 20 minutes.
3. Spray air fryer basket with nonstick spray and place lamb chops in it.
4. Cook at 360°F for approximately 20minutes. This will cook chops to medium. The meat will be juicy but have no remaining pink. Cook for a minute or two longer for well done chops. For rare chops, stop cooking after about 12minutes and check for doneness.

Nutrition Info: Calories per serving: 463; Carbohydrates: 0.2g; Protein: 63.7g; Fat: 21.2g; Sugar: 0g; Sodium: 173mg; Fiber: 0.1g

Tuscan Veal Chops

Servings: 2
Cooking Time: 12-15 Minutes

Ingredients:
- 4 teaspoons Olive oil
- 2 teaspoons Finely minced garlic
- 2 teaspoons Finely minced fresh rosemary leaves
- 1 teaspoon Finely grated lemon zest
- 1 teaspoon Crushed fennel seeds
- 1 teaspoon Table salt
- Up to ¼ teaspoon Red pepper flakes
- 2 10-ounce bone-in veal loin or rib chop(s), about ½ inch thick

Directions:
1. Preheat the air fryer to 400°F.
2. Mix the oil, garlic, rosemary, lemon zest, fennel seeds, salt, and red pepper flakes in a small bowl. Rub this mixture onto both sides of the veal chop(s). Set aside at room temperature as the machine comes to temperature.
3. Set the chop(s) in the basket. If you're cooking more than one chop, leave as much air space between them as possible. Air-fry undisturbed for 12 minutes for medium-rare, or until an instant-read meat thermometer inserted into the center of a chop (without touching bone) registers 135°F (not USDA-approved). Or air-fry undisturbed for 15 minutes for medium-well, or until an instant-read meat thermometer registers 145°F (USDA-approved).
4. Use kitchen tongs to transfer the chops to a cutting board or a wire rack. Cool for 5 minutes before serving.

Nutrition Info: Calories per serving: 545; Carbohydrates: 2.6g; Protein: 53.1g; Fat: 34.8g; Sugar: 0.1g; Sodium: 84mg; Fiber: 1.1g

Garlic And Oregano Lamb Chops

Servings: 4
Cooking Time: 17 Minutes

Ingredients:

- 1½ tablespoons Olive oil
- 1 tablespoon Minced garlic
- 1 teaspoon Dried oregano
- 1 teaspoon Finely minced orange zest
- ¾ teaspoon Fennel seeds
- ¾ teaspoon Table salt
- ¾ teaspoon Ground black pepper
- 6 4-ounce, 1-inch-thick lamb loin chops

Directions:

1. Mix the olive oil, garlic, oregano, orange zest, fennel seeds, salt, and pepper in a large bowl. Add the chops and toss well to coat. Set aside as the air fryer heats, tossing one more time.
2. Preheat the air fryer to 400°F.
3. Set the chops bone side down in the basket (that is, so they stand up on their bony edge) with as much air space between them as possible. Air-fry undisturbed for 14 minutes for medium-rare, or until an instant-read meat thermometer inserted into the thickest part of a chop (without touching bone) registers 132°F (not USDA-approved). Or air-fry undisturbed for 17 minutes for well done, or until an instant-read meat thermometer registers 145°F (USDA-approved).
4. Use kitchen tongs to transfer the chops to a wire rack. Cool for 5 minutes before serving.

Nutrition Info: Calories per serving: 369; Carbohydrates: 1.5g; Protein: 48g; Fat: 17.8g; Sugar: 0g; Sodium: 568mg; Fiber: 0.5g

Marinated Rib-eye Steak With Herb Roasted Mushrooms

Servings: 2
Cooking Time: 10-15 Minutes

Ingredients:

- 2 tablespoons Worcestershire sauce
- ¼ cup red wine
- 2 (8-ounce) boneless rib-eye steaks
- coarsely ground black pepper
- 8 ounces baby bella (cremini) mushrooms, stems trimmed and caps halved
- 2 tablespoons olive oil
- 1 teaspoon dried parsley
- 1 teaspoon fresh thyme leaves
- salt and freshly ground black pepper
- chopped fresh chives or parsley

Directions:

1. Combine the Worcestershire sauce and red wine in a shallow baking dish. Add the steaks to the marinade, pierce them several times with the tines of a fork or a meat tenderizer and season them generously with the coarsely ground black pepper. Flip the steaks over and pierce the other side in a similar fashion, seasoning again with the coarsely ground black pepper. Marinate the steaks for 2 hours.
2. Preheat the air fryer to 400°F.
3. Toss the mushrooms in a bowl with the olive oil, dried parsley, thyme, salt and freshly ground black pepper. Transfer the steaks from the marinade to the air fryer basket, season with salt and scatter the mushrooms on top.
4. Air-fry the steaks for 10 minutes for medium-rare, 12 minutes for medium, or 15 minutes for well-done, flipping the steaks once halfway through the cooking time.
5. Serve the steaks and mushrooms together with the chives or parsley sprinkled on top. A good steak sauce or some horseradish would be a nice accompaniment.

Nutrition Info: Calories per serving: 65; Carbohydrates: 7.9g; Protein: 72.1g; Fat: 36.2g; Sugar: 5.2g; Sodium: 310mg; Fiber: 1.3g

Pork Loin

Servings: 8
Cooking Time: 50 Minutes

Ingredients:
- 1 tablespoon lime juice
- 1 tablespoon sugar-free orange marmalade
- 1 teaspoon coarse brown mustard
- 1 teaspoon curry powder
- 1 teaspoon dried lemongrass
- 2-pound boneless pork loin roast
- salt and pepper
- cooking spray

Directions:
1. Mix together the lime juice, marmalade, mustard, curry powder, and lemongrass.
2. Rub mixture all over the surface of the pork loin. Season to taste with salt and pepper.
3. Spray air fryer basket with nonstick spray and place pork roast diagonally in basket.
4. Cook at 360°F for approximately 50 minutes, until roast registers 130°F on a meat thermometer.
5. Wrap roast in foil and let rest for 10 minutes before slicing.

Nutrition Info: Calories per serving: 164; Carbohydrates: 0.9g; Protein: 29.7g; Fat: 13.1g; Sugar: 0g; Sodium: 84mg; Fiber: 0.1g

T-bone Steak With Roasted Tomato, Corn And Asparagus Salsa

Servings: 4

Cooking Time: 15-20 Minutes

Ingredients:
- 1 (20-ounce) T-bone steak
- salt and freshly ground black pepper
- Salsa
- 1½ cups cherry tomatoes
- ¾ cup corn kernels (fresh, or frozen and thawed)
- 1½ cups sliced asparagus (1-inch slices) (about ½ bunch)
- 1 tablespoon + 1 teaspoon olive oil, divided
- salt and freshly ground black pepper
- 1½ teaspoons red wine vinegar
- 3 tablespoons chopped fresh basil
- 1 tablespoon chopped fresh chives

Directions:

1. Preheat the air fryer to 400°F.
2. Season the steak with salt and pepper and air-fry at 400°F for 10 minutes (medium-rare), 12 minutes (medium), or 15 minutes (well-done), flipping the steak once halfway through the cooking time.
3. In the meantime, toss the tomatoes, corn and asparagus in a bowl with a teaspoon or so of olive oil, salt and freshly ground black pepper.
4. When the steak has finished cooking, remove it to a cutting board, tent loosely with foil and let it rest. Transfer the vegetables to the air fryer and air-fry at 400°F for 5 minutes, shaking the basket once or twice during the cooking process. Transfer the cooked vegetables back into the bowl and toss with the red wine vinegar, remaining olive oil and fresh herbs.
5. To serve, slice the steak on the bias and serve with some of the salsa on top.

Nutrition Info: Calories per serving: 424; Carbohydrates: 15.6g; Protein: 31.8g; Fat: 25g; Sugar: 7g; Sodium: 184mg; Fiber: 4g

Cinnamon-stick Kofta Skewers

Servings: 4
Cooking Time: 15 Minutes

Ingredients:

- 1 pound Lean ground beef
- ½ teaspoon Ground cumin
- ½ teaspoon Onion powder
- ½ teaspoon Ground dried turmeric
- ½ teaspoon Ground cinnamon
- ½ teaspoon Table salt
- Up to a ⅛ teaspoon Cayenne
- 8 3½- to 4-inch-long cinnamon sticks (see the headnote)
- Vegetable oil spray

Directions:

1. Preheat the air fryer to 375°F.
2. Gently mix the ground beef, cumin, onion powder, turmeric, cinnamon, salt, and cayenne in a bowl until the meat is evenly mixed with the spices. (Clean, dry hands work best!) Divide this mixture into 2-ounce portions, each about the size of a golf ball.
3. Wrap one portion of the meat mixture around a cinnamon stick, using about three-quarters of the length of the stick, covering one end but leaving a little "handle" of cinnamon stick protruding from the other end. Set aside and continue making more kofta skewers.
4. Generously coat the formed kofta skewers on all sides with vegetable oil spray. Set them in the basket with as much air space between them as possible. Air-fry undisturbed for 13 minutes, or until browned and cooked through. If the machine is at 360°F, you may need to add 2 minutes to the cooking time.
5. Use a nonstick-safe spatula, and perhaps kitchen tongs for balance, to gently transfer the kofta skewers to a wire rack. Cool for at least 5 minutes or up to 20 minutes before serving.

Nutrition Info: Calories per serving: 213; Carbohydrates: 0.6g; Protein: 34.5g; Fat: 7.1g; Sugar: 0.1g; Sodium: 366mg; Fiber: 0.2g

Flank Steak With Roasted Peppers And Chimichurri

Servings: 4
Cooking Time: 22 Minutes

Ingredients:

- 2 cups flat-leaf parsley leaves
- ¼ cup fresh oregano leaves
- 3 cloves garlic
- ½ cup olive oil
- ¼ cup red wine vinegar
- ½ teaspoon salt
- freshly ground black pepper
- ¼ teaspoon crushed red pepper flakes
- ½ teaspoon ground cumin
- 1 pound flank steak
- 1 red bell pepper, cut into strips
- 1 yellow bell pepper, cut into strips

Directions:

1. Make the chimichurri sauce by chopping the parsley, oregano and garlic in a food processor. Add the olive oil, vinegar and seasonings and process again. Pour half of the sauce into a shallow dish with the flank steak and set the remaining sauce aside. Pierce the flank steak with a needle-style meat tenderizer or a paring knife and marinate the steak for 2 to 24 hours in the refrigerator. When you are ready to cook, remove the steak from the refrigerator and let it sit at room temperature for 30 minutes.
2. Preheat the air fryer to 400°F.
3. Cut the flank steak in half so that it fits more easily into the air fryer and transfer both pieces to the air fryer basket. Air-fry for 14 minutes, depending on how you like your steak cooked (10 minutes will give you medium for a 1-inch thick flank steak). Flip the steak over halfway through the cooking time.
4. When the flank steak is cooked to your liking, transfer it to a cutting board, loosely tent with foil and let it rest while you cook the peppers.
5. Toss the peppers in a little olive oil, salt and freshly ground black pepper and transfer them to the air fryer basket. Air-fry at 400°F for 8 minutes, shaking the basket once or twice throughout the cooking process. To serve, slice the flank steak against the grain of the meat and top with the roasted peppers. Drizzle the reserved chimichurri sauce on top, thinning the sauce with another tablespoon of olive oil if desired.

Nutrition Info: Calories per serving: 480; Carbohydrates: 8.6g; Protein: 33.7g; Fat: 35.5g; Sugar: 2g; Sodium: 375mg; Fiber: 4g

Lollipop Lamb Chops With Mint Pesto

Servings: 4

Cooking Time: 7 Minutes

Ingredients:

- Mint Pesto
- ½ small clove garlic
- ¼ cup packed fresh parsley
- ¾ cup packed fresh mint
- ½ teaspoon lemon juice
- ¼ cup grated Parmesan cheese
- ⅓ cup shelled pistachios
- ¼ teaspoon salt
- ½ cup olive oil
- 8 "frenched" lamb chops (1 rack)
- olive oil
- salt and freshly ground black pepper
- 1 tablespoon dried rosemary, chopped
- 1 tablespoon dried thyme

Directions:

1. Make the pesto by combining the garlic, parsley and mint in a food processor and process until finely chopped. Add the lemon juice, Parmesan cheese, pistachios and salt. Process until all the ingredients have turned into a paste. With the processor running, slowly pour the olive oil in through the feed tube. Scrape the sides of the processor with a spatula and process for another 30 seconds.
2. Preheat the air fryer to 400°F.
3. Rub both sides of the lamb chops with olive oil and season with salt, pepper, rosemary and thyme, pressing the herbs into the meat gently with your fingers. Transfer the lamb chops to the air fryer basket.
4. Air-fry the lamb chops at 400°F for 5 minutes. Flip the chops over and air-fry for an additional 2 minutes. This should bring the chops to a medium-rare doneness, depending on their thickness. Adjust the cooking time up or down a minute or two accordingly for different degrees of doneness.
5. Serve the lamb chops with mint pesto drizzled on top.

Nutrition Info: Calories per serving: 560; Carbohydrates: 4g; Protein: 38.4g; Fat: 44.1g; Sugar: 0.4g; Sodium: 346mg; Fiber: 2.4g

Venison Backstrap

Servings: 4
Cooking Time: 10 Minutes

Ingredients:
- 2 eggs
- ¼ cup milk
- 1 cup whole wheat flour
- ½ teaspoon salt
- ¼ teaspoon pepper
- 1 pound venison backstrap, sliced
- salt and pepper
- oil for misting or cooking spray

Directions:
1. Beat together eggs and milk in a shallow dish.
2. In another shallow dish, combine the flour, salt, and pepper. Stir to mix well.
3. Sprinkle venison steaks with additional salt and pepper to taste. Dip in flour, egg wash, then in flour again, pressing in coating.
4. Spray steaks with oil or cooking spray on both sides.
5. Cooking in 2 batches, place steaks in the air fryer basket in a single layer. Cook at 360°F for 8minutes. Spray with oil, turn over, and spray other side. Cook for 2 minutes longer, until coating is crispy brown and meat is done to your liking.
6. Repeat to cook remaining venison.

Nutrition Info: Calories per serving: 297; Carbohydrates: 19g; Protein: 33.2g; Fat: 4.6g; Sugar: 0.9g; Sodium: 329mg; Fiber: 4g

Perfect Strip Steaks

Servings: 2

Cooking Time: 17 Minutes

Ingredients:
- 1½ tablespoons Olive oil
- 1½ tablespoons Minced garlic
- 2 teaspoons Ground black pepper
- 1 teaspoon Table salt
- 2 (¾-pound) boneless beef strip steak(s)

Directions:
1. Preheat the air fryer to 375°F (or 380°F or 390°F, if one of these is the closest setting).
2. Mix the oil, garlic, pepper, and salt in a small bowl, then smear this mixture over both sides of the steak(s).
3. When the machine is at temperature, put the steak(s) in the basket with as much air space as possible between them for the larger batch. They should not overlap or even touch. That said, even just a ¼-inch between them will work. Air-fry for 12 minutes, turning once, until an instant-read meat thermometer inserted into the thickest part of a steak registers 127°F for rare (not USDA-approved). Or air-fry for 15 minutes, turning once, until an instant-read meat thermometer registers 145°F for medium (USDA-approved). If the machine is at 390°F, the steaks may cook 2 minutes more quickly than the stated timing.
4. Use kitchen tongs to transfer the steak(s) to a wire rack. Cool for 5 minutes before serving.

Nutrition Info: Calories per serving: 840; Carbohydrates: 3.4g; Protein: 103.3g; Fat: 13.1g; Sugar: 0.1g; Sodium: 840mg; Fiber: 0.7g

Smokehouse-style Beef Ribs

Servings: 3
Cooking Time: 25 Minutes

Ingredients:
- ¼ teaspoon Mild smoked paprika
- ¼ teaspoon Garlic powder
- ¼ teaspoon Onion powder
- ¼ teaspoon Table salt
- ¼ teaspoon Ground black pepper
- 3 10- to 12-ounce beef back ribs (not beef short ribs)

Directions:
1. Preheat the air fryer to 350°F.
2. Mix the smoked paprika, garlic powder, onion powder, salt, and pepper in a small bowl until uniform. Massage and pat this mixture onto the ribs.
3. When the machine is at temperature, set the ribs in the basket in one layer, turning them on their sides if necessary, sort of like they're spooning but with at least ¼ inch air space between them. Air-fry for 25 minutes, turning once, until deep brown and sizzling.
4. Use kitchen tongs to transfer the ribs to a wire rack. Cool for 5 minutes before serving.

Nutrition Info: Calories per serving: 635; Carbohydrates: 0.6g; Protein: 74.8g; Fat: 33.1g; Sugar: 0.2g; Sodium: 394mg; Fiber: 0.2g

Peppered Steak Bites

Servings: 4
Cooking Time: 14 Minutes

Ingredients:
- 1 pound sirloin steak, cut into 1-inch cubes
- ½ teaspoon coarse sea salt
- 1 teaspoon coarse black pepper
- 2 teaspoons Worcestershire sauce
- ½ teaspoon garlic powder
- ¼ teaspoon red pepper flakes
- ¼ cup chopped parsley

Directions:
1. Preheat the air fryer to 390°F.
2. In a large bowl, place the steak cubes and toss with the salt, pepper, Worcestershire sauce, garlic powder, and red pepper flakes.
3. Pour the steak into the air fryer basket and cook for 10 to 14 minutes, depending on how well done you prefer your bites. Starting at the 8-minute mark, toss the steak bites every 2 minutes to check for doneness.
4. When the steak is cooked, remove it from the basket to a serving bowl and top with the chopped parsley. Allow the steak to rest for 5 minutes before serving.

Nutrition Info: Calories per serving: 217; Carbohydrates: 1.4g; Protein: 34.6g; Fat: 7.1g; Sugar: 0.6g; Sodium: 339mg; Fiber: 0.3g

Lamb Koftas Meatballs

Servings: 3
Cooking Time: 8 Minutes

Ingredients:
- 1 pound ground lamb
- 1 teaspoon ground cumin
- 1 teaspoon ground coriander
- 2 tablespoons chopped fresh mint
- 1 egg, beaten
- ½ teaspoon salt
- freshly ground black pepper

Directions:

1. Combine all ingredients in a bowl and mix together well. Divide the mixture into 10 portions. Roll each portion into a ball and then by cupping the meatball in your hand, shape it into an oval.
2. Preheat the air fryer to 400°F.
3. Air-fry the koftas for 8 minutes.
4. Serve warm with the cucumber-yogurt dip.

Nutrition Info: Calories per serving: 307; Carbohydrates: 0.7g; Protein: 44.6g; Fat: 12.7g; Sugar: 0.1g; Sodium: 525mg; Fiber: 0.3g

Printed in Great Britain
by Amazon